1943

PLAIN
PUBLIC
SPEAKING

Charles R. Gruner
The University of Georgia

MACMILLAN PUBLISHING CO., INC.
New York

COLLIER MACMILLAN PUBLISHERS
London

Macmillan Publishing Co., Inc.
866 Third Avenue, New York, New York 10022

Collier Macmillan Canada, Ltd.

Library of Congress Cataloging in Publication Data

Gruner, Charles R.
   Plain public speaking.

   Bibliography: p. 181
   Includes index.
   1. Public speaking.   I. Title.
PN4121.G76   808.5′1   82-15300
ISBN 0-02-348340-7   AACR2

Printing: 6 7 8   Year: 8 9 0

ISBN   0-02-348340-7

To Marsha, Mark, and Valerie, who always speak plainly—
And especially to Mom.

PREFACE

Years ago a great football coach said on television something to the effect that "Great football teams stick to the basics. Usually a game is won by the team that does the best job of blocking and tackling."

My intention has been to write a book that sticks to teaching the basics—the "blocking and tackling"—of public speaking. Because if you will stick to the basics presented, and put in enough work on them for each speaking endeavor, you may not win the acclaim of all your compatriots, but you won't lose very often, either.

Over the years I have found that beginning speakers who will deliberately, ploddingly follow the eight-step formula presented in Chapter 2 (the basic "blocking and tackling" chapter) for each speech assignment successfully achieve their goals in terms of audience response. And I have found that students who attempt to short-circuit or circumvent the eight-step formula fail in varying degrees to inform or persuade their listeners.

To help you create speeches with the eight-step formula I have provided information in these chapters to calm your fears and to tell you how to find and use good content, organization, style of language and vocal and visible delivery. Chapter 8 addresses the special problems of composing a speech to convey information to an audience and Chapter 9 does the same for persuasion.

I assume that you have this book in your hands because you want to become a (better?) public speaker. If you will let this book help you, you *will!* Good luck.

CONTENTS

1

So You Have to Give a Speech (or Have a Speech to Give)

THE
SPEECH

Do you have to give a speech? Or, have you a speech to give? If so, do you believe it will be a *good* speech? You may doubt that it will. After all, when was the last time you *heard* a really good speech? Of all the many speeches you must have heard in the past few years, has there been *one* that lifted your heart? Inspired you to action? Dazzled you with an original thought? Gave you a new and exciting slant on an old idea? Taught you a useful skill or concept? And at the same time held your attention as if in a vise?

Chances are, you cannot remember hearing such a speech—because you haven't. But if you are one of the fortunate few who have heard a good speech and had your pulse quickened, your blood pressure raised, and your mind aroused, you will have a vivid memory of it.

Most public speeches you have been exposed to have probably been pretty drab and dreary. Why? Well, there are several reasons.

First, most speeches are made by people who have not been especially trained to make speeches. They make speeches because they are asked to or because they have a certain position or area of expertise, not because they are good speakers. People are asked to speak because they are businesspeople, lawyers, doctors, politicians, or college deans; because they grow the best roses in town or bake the best cake or have written a book. In short, they speak because of who they are, not because of how well they speak.

Second, people often do a poor job at speaking because, once they have agreed to speak, they simply refuse to do the hard work it takes to create an effective speech. And giving a truly good speech does take work—and time. Lafcadio Hearn once affirmed that "All the best work is done the way ants do things—by tiny but untiring and regular additions." Few people imitate the ants.

As a speech teacher, I am literally baffled by people who seem to take the attitude that a good speech can be cranked out with a bare minimum of time and energy. These same people are well aware that a lot of painstaking travail is necessary to create an effective written essay, a beautiful painting, a haunting poem, an entertaining musical performance, a successful advertising campaign, or a professional-looking woodcarving. Their attitude seems to be "Heck, speaking is easy. I been talking all my life!"

A cynic says, "Work is fascinating; I can watch it for hours!" Too bad so many would-be speakers take the same attitude. The result is bad speeches. And any speaker who gives a bad twenty-minute speech to two hundred people has wasted over sixty hours of audience time. That is criminal.

So if you are reading this book right now and are not willing to make the effort and do the work and take the time to do your best at speech making, do not expect the rewards and the genuine satisfaction of speeches made truly well. Mediocre speaking is easy; good speaking is not.

Another major reason for poor public speaking is egocentricity, both positive and negative.

Positive egocentricity manifests itself in the speaker's complete obliviousness to the agony being suffered by the poor audience. Such a speaker parades self-satisfaction, personal virtues, and abstract, foggy ideas before an audience about whom she or he could not care less. The speaker is self-centered, not audience-centered. Such a speaker reminds one of the philosophy professor who, while lecturing, peered to the back of the room. "Who's smoking back there?" he demanded. A student replied, "Nobody. That's just the fog we're in."

I once had the misfortune of having in one of my college classes a young man who had taken one of those expensive private courses billed as a "public speaking" course but really designed to do little but plump up the customer's self-image. For his assignment to "introduce himself" for one to two minutes before the class, this student wearied his classmates into a near stupor with personal trivia for nearly twenty minutes. He might have gone on for the entire period, but I stepped in to save the class from going comatose. I spent the entire quarter in a futile attempt to convince that young man that he was *not* the greatest orator since Winston Churchill.

Negative egocentricity takes the form of what we call stage fright (and what modern "scholars" have obscured with the name *communication apprehension*). The novice speaker, obviously scared spitless, shivers and stammers through a pitiful self-directed monologue. Through the process of empathy, the audience picks up the speaker's nervous misery. Everyone is as uncomfortable as sinners in church, and the whole affair is a fiasco.

Chapter 3 will take a stab at helping you overcome *negative* egocentricity. However, this book will make no attempt to counsel you on excessive *positive* egocentricity. No one has yet discovered how to reform a bore. (Bore: one who talks when you want him or her to listen.)

So much public speaking resembles anesthesiology without medical licensing because many speeches are read from a cold, lifeless manuscript. And all too often, the speech manuscript was not even written by the speaker, but by an aide or other hireling. And very few speakers possess the talent or the training to breathe life into a manuscript into which all the thinking was put days or weeks ago (maybe by someone else). So the speaker reads the thing word for word (which any literate eight-year-old could do) without even *listening* to those words, occasionally making hilarious (and unconscious) blunders; from this practice we get our famous radio and television "bloopers" ("General Marshall arrived at the conference tall, dignified, and uninformed").

There you have it. Most public speaking is simply goshawful because (1) speakers are not trained; (2) they are lazy; (3) they suffer (as do their audiences) from positive or negative egocentricity; and/or (4) they read bloodless "essays on their hind legs."

So, if you are willing to follow the training tips in this book; if you are willing to work; if you can personally incorporate Chapter 3's advice on stage fright; and if you will dare to learn to speak without the crutch of a manuscript, you can become a good mind-appeal speaker (provided, of course, that you have a modicum of intelligence and vocal equipment in reasonably good repair).

I use the term *mind-appeal speaker* deliberately to distinguish between the kind of speaker that can be *made* from the kind that must be *born*—the kind that columnist Jenkin Lloyd Jones calls the *haranguer*. No one can be *trained* to become a great haranguer, such as Cuba's Fidel Castro or the late Gamal Abdul Nasser of Egypt or the late Senator Huey Long of Louisiana. These men are (or were) mystical, hypnotic speakers, able to rant and rave for hours without making one bit of sense. But these haranguers could sway their hordes of followers the way the westerlies can the Iowa wheat fields. No, you cannot be trained to become one of these. But with the right attitude, you can be trained to speak with eminent good sense.

And let us consider this matter of "attitude" before plunging into the seven-step formula for speech preparation in Chapter 2.

Return for a moment to the title of this chapter and its first sentence, for those two questions represents a profound difference in the attitudes that a speaker can take toward the speaking situation.

If you are taking a course in speech, it may be that you see each assigned speech as "just an assignment." Each time, you will have the attitude "I have to give a speech." Each speech will be related to drudgery, apprehension, and perhaps even terror. And chances are, you will give a poor speech.

If, however, you can adopt the view for each assignment, "I have a speech to give!" a whole new attitude surfaces. You are telling yourself, "I have a worthwhile message for this audience." You will accept each "assignment" as an opportunity to communicate information and ideas to your fellows. You will approach the job positively, exuding energy and industriousness, looking forward to the moment when the podium is yours. You will present your speech with your natural earnestness and enthusiasm; the audience will pick up your robustness through the process of empathy. Both you and your audience will enjoy the experience. And get a lot out of it.

This difference in attitude can make all the difference in the world. As C. G. Jung said, "It all depends on how we look at things, and not on how they are in themselves." That's why the pessimist can see a glass that is half empty and the optimist can see one that is half full.

Get Off
Square One

In his nightclub act, comedian Mort Sahl used to remark that just before being hanged as an American spy in the Revolution, Nathan Hale said, "I only regret that I have but one life to lose for my country." However, Sahl quipped, when shot down in his U-2 spy plane and captured by the Russians, Francis Gary Powers muttered, "This destroys all my plans."

Well, plans are important. Probably no significant human endeavor is successful unless it is preceded by careful and systematic planning. Buildings are not thrown up overnight, for instance, but proceed through calculated stages. The building's purpose must be determined; a site must be selected; an architect draws up blueprints; bids are secured; materials are purchased; and so on.

This chapter presents a plan of seven systematic steps that can lead to successful speaking. Follow it carefully, dutifully, step-by-step, for each speech you prepare. Eventually, when you become an experienced speaker, you will incorporate these seven steps into your speech preparation without conscious awareness of them, slipping from one to another, back and forth, as the need arises. But for now take them chronologically and deliberately, as presented. Here they are:

1. Choose your topic.

2. Decide on and write down your specific purpose, or goal, in terms of *audience response.*

3. Decide which main points, or ideas, you must get across to your audience in order to achieve your specific purpose or goal.

4. Assemble all the material you already know that can be used to prove or illustrate each of your main points.

5. Gather further supporting materials not already at hand that support your main points.

6. Cast the assembled materials into an outline.

7. Rehearse from the outline, in a realistic manner, until you are satisfied that you can do a good job of delivering it.

Now let's take up each of these steps in detail.

Choosing Your Topic. For the expert, this is easy. For the young beginner in a course, it can be tough.

The expert, by definition, already *has* a topic. The lawyer can speak on the new DUI law; the doctor can speak on cardiac arrest; the first-aid instructor can talk on and demonstrate the Heimlich maneuver or CPR; the ardent hiker can speak on experiences along the Appalachian Trail. In fact, the expert is usually asked to speak on a particular topic of expertise; in "real life," the speaker is, in effect, *assigned* a topic.

But the most common question of the young speech student is, "But what can I talk on?"

What this question really indicates is "I do not already have a prepared speech of the proper length that meets the requirements of the assignment." Most students really do have topics on which they can speak. They just need to go to the bother of converting them from "topics" to speeches.

Select a topic on which to speak that is already familiar. Almost everyone has some special interest: a hobby, a subject on which a term paper was successfully written, a skill or concept learned in scouts or athletics, an interest picked up from a book. If you will sit down and take a careful inventory of your own apperceptive mass, you can probably come up with a number of topics on which you have some knowledge or strong opinion and on which you could speak at some future time. If such an inventory really does come up blank, then you had really better forego public speaking or else take some steps to fill your head with some subject matter. If you have an empty bucket you need to find a well. In this world, only well-informed people are asked to speak in public.

Choose a topic that will suit your audience. It should be something they will find useful, or interesting, or entertaining. If your speech is a persuasive one, your topic should be one that can be made convincing to them. Again, if you are the invited expert, you have no problem. The audience doing the inviting is presumably already agreed that your topic is suitable for them. However, if you are a student in a course, you need to analyze your audience to determine what would be a good topic for them (or how a particular topic can be *made* suitable to them). Because those in the audience, your fellow students, are apt to be quite similar to yourself, you might begin by asking yourself, "What would *I* like to hear a speech on?" (or, "What would I *not* like to hear a speech on?"). We will take up audience analysis again in Chapters 8 and 9.

Deciding on Your Specific Purpose or Goal. All good speeches are clearly purposeful, that is, goal-oriented. A good speech seeks a specific audience response and is focused directly on obtaining that response. Most poor speeches are unclear in this regard.

Choosing the specific response you want from the audience is a most important step, for it determines all else that follows in your preparation.

The speaker with a clear goal is like the purposeful traveler, who first determines his or her destination. Maps are brought out, routes are chosen, driving times are calculated. Possible stops for food and gasoline are determined. Costs are figured. Clothes for the trip are selected.

Likewise, the speaker with a clear goal can make purposeful, systematic plans. Given this goal, what main points must be made in order to achieve it? What information do you need to include, and what information can you safely leave out?

The general goals or purposes of a speech are to entertain, to inform, and to persuade. Specific goals tell what you want to achieve in your speech: "My goal is to teach this audience how to administer the Heimlich maneuver"; "My goal is to provide an interesting, entertaining twenty-minute program with my slides of the Appalachian Trail"; "My purpose is to convince the audience that nuclear power is safe"; "My goal is to actuate the members of my audience to give blood during next Tuesday's Red Cross drive."

A speaker without such a clear-cut, specific goal is less like the purposeful traveler and more like the Sunday driver. The Sunday driver has no particular destination in mind; has no estimated time of arrival and no set time to return home; does not know which roads will eventually be taken; and thus becomes an obstruction to the purposeful driver.

Some speakers have as their goal merely "giving a speech."

Like the Sunday driver, such a speaker does not know how the audience will respond to the speech; may not know exactly what will be said in the speech (or may not know why certain material was included in the speech); will not know exactly how long the speech will last; and so on. And such a speaker is usually a crashing bore. Even if not, the audience may walk away thinking, "That was kind of interesting, but what was the speaker really getting at?" Many such speakers are merely like the dry old professor of philosophy: he made his students feel numb on one end and dumb on the other. Others are more like the airline pilot whose voice came over the cabin loudspeakers: "Ladies and gentlemen, I have some bad news and some good news. The bad news is that we are lost; the good news is that we have caught a tailwind and are making very good time."

Deciding on Your Main Points.   If you have in mind a clear goal in terms of audience response, and you already know something about your speech topic, this step should be as easy as falling off a log. The main ideas you must get across to accomplish your goal should be obvious. For instance, you want to teach them the Heimlich maneuver. Then you need to get the following points across to your audience:

1. You must be able to tell the victim of a clogged windpipe from a heart attack victim. The symptoms are . . .

2. You must act quickly to remove the obstruction. Do it in this manner . . .

3. Please understand that this maneuver almost always works because . . .

Do you wish to convince your audience that a new school bond issue should be passed? Then you must convince them that:

1. Our present school's physical plant is (outdated, obsolete, overcrowded, etc.).

2. A new bond issue, if passed, would bring the plant up to par.

3. The new bond issue is the most practical method of improving the school.

Do you plan to actuate your audience members to give blood? Then you need to make these points:

1. There is a pressing need for whole blood.
2. You can help satisfy this need (and your own unselfish desire to be a charitable and a good citizen).
3. Donating blood is painless and fun, and it makes you quietly proud of yourself.

A mosquito found its way into a nudist colony. "Gee," it said to itself, "I have an idea of what I want to do, but I just don't know where to start." If you have a clear idea of the goal you seek in terms of audience response, you will not be confused like that mosquito; you will be able to decide just what major steps to begin on.

Assembling the Supporting Materials You Have.   You know your specific purpose and which main points you need to make in order to accomplish it. Now you need to assemble the material you already possess that will help get across those main points.

Sit down with pen and paper. Write down every specific fact, figure, comparison, and example that you already know that will help flesh out your speech. It is usually a good idea to put one fact, example, and so on on one note card. Then, later, you can shuffle and reshuffle as your organize your speech into final form. One item per card also makes it easier to add and remove items from the final version of the speech.

As you write down each item of support, make it as specific as possible. In casual conversation, it is all right to say things like "Several years ago when I was out West . . ." or "Firemen around here make pretty good money, considering . . ." But in a speech you need to be accurate and precise: "In 1976 when I was in Tuscon, Arizona . . ." and "Firemen in our city get a starting salary of $14,200 per year . . ." If you cannot be this precise as you record your items of information, you need to do some checking to sharpen them up. This can be done during the next step.

Gathering Additional Supporting Material.   It is hardly conceivable that you will have all the information needed to flesh out your main points into a successful speech without going outside your own nervous system. You will need to do some research.

Research usually means library work. If you have access to a good college library, you are in luck. You may not know how to find the right kind of information there, however. In that case, you need to get over to the library and find out how to use it. The material in Chapter 4 can help you.

The most important thing to be stressed here is that research is *necessary*, and you must adopt the attitude that you will *do* it. It may be that you will be able to enchant an audience with no other material than what you can churn up out of your own head, but I seriously doubt it.

There is also research other than library research. Are there any experts on your topic in your town whom you could visit or interview on the phone? Is there a company nearby that is likely to have information they would provide you because it is in their own best interest to do so? (For instance, the power company can probably give you some material on insulation or nuclear fission; a local beverage plant will have information on aluminum and glass recycling; your hospital will have brochures on CPR and blood donating.) Do you have any books in your home to which you can turn, such as a good encyclopedia, a copy of the *Guinness Book of World Records,* a good dictionary, or a paperback *Statistical Abstract* (available at most newstands)?

Here let me stress: *Gather far more material than you will be able to use in your speech.* Fill yourself full of your subject; assure yourself, thereby, that you know your subject backward and forward. Remember, an expert preparing a speech has more trouble deciding what to leave out of that speech than deciding what to leave in. You should try to reconstruct this ideal situation. The actual amount of material you use in your speech should relate to how much you know on your topic in about the same way that the tip of an iceberg relates to how much of it is under water.

Outlining.   After you have gathered far more than enough material for your speech, with one point per card, divide your cards up according to which main point each supports. Then create an outline of your speech in which your main points are separated and each has its subpoints and support indented and recorded under it. You will find more details on outlining in Chapter 5. After your main points and support are properly outlined, you can begin work on a good introduction and a conclusion to your speech. But this outline is designed for one particular purpose: to rehearse from.

It is during the process of outlining, also, that you can begin to pick and choose from among your supporting materials from the piles of cards you have accumulated. Since you have only one point per card, it should be physically easy to winnow out the best of the lot, even though it may be emotionally difficult to discard the fruits of your labor.

Rehearsing.   So far, we have been mostly considering pretty mechanical spadework on a speech. Now we come to an area that becomes more creative and less mechanical. And different people approach it in different ways.

Some people go over and over the outline orally, changing the specific wording each time, perhaps, but learning the sequence of ideas nonetheless. Most who do it this way generally stop rehearsing once they have gone through it several times and are satisfied with their delivery. Learning the speech this way is ideal; you learn the sequence of ideas. Then, when you present the actual speech, the appropriate ideas come to mind in order, and you clothe these ideas in your own conversational language, choosing your words as you think the thought. Assured, conversational speaking is the result, coming naturally in an easy, oral style.

Others speak the outline into a tape recorder one or more times, then copy the speech from the recorder in written form; the copy is then edited and polished. The final manuscript is then rehearsed orally over and over until it becomes second nature to the speaker. This is a good way to ensure that any written manuscript the speaker uses will retain a more oral style than a manuscript written from scratch. It was spoken first and written last, not vice versa.

Some speakers go right from an outline to a written manuscript, which is then edited, rehearsed, and polished. This technique is more likely to result in what sounds like an "essay on its hind legs" because of the written nature of the style. (See Chapter 6).

The preferred method is the first one mentioned; this is the "extemporaneous" method and results, usually, in the most communication between speaker and listener. If you really *must* use a manuscript, the second method is recommended.

No doubt your speech (whether "assigned" or "invited") will entail some sort of time limit. For this and other reasons, your rehearsals must be as realistic as possible. If the speech turns out to be too long, you will have to squeeze some of the material out; if it comes out short, you will have to add more material. By *realistic* rehearsal I mean several things:

1. Rehearse the speech standing up and out loud. Sitting at your desk reading over your note cards is not rehearsal. It is studying or "preparation" of some sort, but it is not rehearsing to familiarize yourself with the actual event.

2. Rehearse with whatever materials you will use in your real presentation. Are you using 35mm slides? Have them in each rehearsal. Using charts? The blackboard? A flannel board? An overhead projector? Charts or graphs? Rehearse with them, too. Eventually, have a dress rehearsal or two; wear the actual clothes you will wear for the speech.

3. Rehearse in a room of the same size and type as the room in which you will speak. Can you get over to and into the actual room in which you will speak, at least for the last rehearsal or two? It would be a good idea to do so; then when you give your speech, you will not feel as if it's the first time you have done it.

4. Perhaps most important: rehearse before an audience as much as you can. Get your spouse, your friends, your secretary, your roommates to listen to your speech. Get their remarks by way of feedback. Did they understand it? Were they confused by anything you said? Were they persuaded? Did you look and sound OK to them? Did any of your mannerisms bug them? Did your clothes look appropriate?

An incident occurred in one of my classes that brought thudding home to me the necessity of rehearsing before a real audience. An attractive young woman was to give her persuasive speech on a warm Friday afternoon. Because of the day and time, several students were absent, including all but one other woman.

The student had chosen the delicate subject "Marijuana Will Ruin Your Sex Life!" Included as part of her argument were the interesting results of a California study in which college males volunteered to smoke six joints a day and measure the relevant effects. Approaching the essence of the report, she began to show an increasingly embarrassed awareness that her audience was composed almost exclusively of the opposite sex and that her topic, however objectively she presented it, was susceptible to interpretation by innuendo. She managed to force herself to a conclusion, but it was a faltering one with a shattered delivery.

Afterward I asked her if she had rehearsed the speech. She had, but only to her female roommate. She had not foreseen the difficulty of presenting her topic to a virtually undiluted masculine audience.

So these are the seven sure-fire steps to follow systematically in preparing a speech for delivery. Remember them. Follow them. Each time you begin work on a speech, review these steps. Avoid shortcuts, for in them lie pitfalls.

Speak Without Fear and Trembling

In 1973 a poll was conducted to find out what Americans feared most. Results: topping the list was the fear of giving a speech in public. Farther down on the list were fear of heights and fear of *death!* This will give you an idea of how widespread "stage fright" is.

Some speech teachers (and speech books) say very little about stage fright. These teachers notice that it tends to diminish as speech students get a little experience, so they figure, "Why bring up that nasty subject?" What such teachers do not take into account is that their students tend to get over the fear of speaking to that particular classroom of folks, but that when new audience situations come up later, stage fright once again increases to uncomfortable levels.

One class of people you might expect not to suffer the shakes, gasps, and chills of stage fright would be college speech professors. Not true. Why, back in 1969 at a meeting of my national professional association, I saw two such profs, both friends of mine, get so scared while reporting on their research that they passed out cold! Not only is stage fright shared by all universally, but it persists over a lifetime.

The first step in coping with any psychological problem is to [try to understand it. That is] just what we are going to attempt in [this chapter. Let's look] at the *symptoms* of stage fright.

[Stage] fright is a fear reaction. And all fear [has a certain] kind of symptoms. Everyone has been [afraid, so] you will recognize these fear reaction [symptoms.]

[When you recogn]ize a danger, you feel a sudden spasm [... adr]enaline. This is what Hans Selye called the "alarm reaction." If this danger persists, your body undergoes a number of changes.

Your heart begins pounding harder. You might be reminded of Poe's story "The Tell-Tale Heart." You become breathless; your breath comes and goes in little short pants. Your face flushes. The palms of your hands and the soles of your feet break out in a cold sweat (you literally get "cold feet"). There is a sinking sensation in your stomach (some call this butterflies). Your mouth goes dry and cottony. You find it difficult to control your voice; it feels as if it will break, squeak, croak. Your mind starts going blank ("The human brain is a marvelous organ; begins working the day you are born and doesn't quit until you get up to give a speech."). You find yourself trembling, especially in the extremities: your hands, arms, and legs. Your skin may break out in goosebumps.

All these symptoms become disconcerting if your task is to give a speech. So what do you do? Well, you feel pretty awkward, don't you? You can't find a comfortable way to stand. You shift from one foot to another, hoping the trembling in your knees will subside. Your arms and hands feel oversized and not firmly under your control. So you fidget with a pencil or a button or your ear. You try to hide your hands behind you, in pockets, or behind the lectern, or you cross your arms. You try to avoid the audience by not looking at them. You look down at the lectern, out the window, at the ceiling—anywhere but at those *faces* out there. You try to talk as fast as possible in order to get finished that much sooner. Your numbed brain may not be able to keep up with your racing words, so you fill all blank spots with *uh*'s and *um*'s and *you know*'s.

Why does all this happen? Why is your body running ninety miles an hour when you really would like to have it back at idling speed? There is a very good reason for all this to be happening.

Each of your automatic physiological reactions, controlled by the autonomic nervous system, occurs for a very particular and important reason. Exert yourself or enter a warm room, and you will begin to perspire. The reason? Your body is trying to cool itself down through evaporation. If you get overly chilled, you begin to *shiver*. Why? Your body is rapidly operating your muscles to prompt blood circulation in order to warm itself up. Enter a darkened room and your eye pupils dilate to let in more light; step out into the sunshine and those pupils contract to adjust to the greater light.

What is the reason your body energizes itself when faced with danger? Simple. To prepare you to cope with that danger.

What danger? Well, before humans went and got themselves so civilized, and formed societies like cities and states and nations, and hired soldiers and cops and firefighters to protect them from danger, they had to face danger on their own—and often.

Early, primitive people had to cope with natural disasters like forest fires, volcanic eruptions, lightning, and earthquakes. They had to learn to perform dangerous feats like fording (or swimming) rivers and climbing mountains in order to hunt game for food. They had to fight to protect their territory, their homes, or their families. And they constantly had to be on guard against predatory wild animals.

Coping with any of these dangers would be easier if one had extra strength and energy. And those ancestors of ours who lived long enough to pass on their genes to us were those who developed the fear syndrome of symptoms, which, taken together, add up to extra strength and energy.

Let us consider one of those ancient ancestors, a primordial man plodding along some Old World path. Rounding a turn in the path, he comes face-to-face with a saber-toothed tiger!

What can this guy do to keep from being the tiger's lunch? Can he change colors, as can the chameleon, thus becoming invisible? Nope. Can he talk the tiger into seeking out a plumper, more tender victim for its meal? Never. Can he outwit the tiger in a blinding display of human genius? Hardly.

Our caveman has only two options: he can flee, or he can fight. For either of these activities he needs extra strength, endurance, and energy. And if he is one of those who survived to produce progeny, his system for getting through emergencies operated.

While the adrenaline flow provided his first instant burst of energy, his autonomic nervous system clanged into action. It ordered the heart to begin circulating blood rapidly and the liver to release a reserve form of energy called *glycogen*, which must be oxidized into energy. Oxidation requires air, so your autonomic nervous system switches your breathing apparatus into high gear. As glycogen is oxidized in the panting lungs, it is pumped out as quick energy to the muscles that will be required to run and/or fight. These muscles, primarily in the arms and the legs, become overly energized. These muscles are set up in antagonistic muscle-pair systems, with one set of muscles on one side of an arm or leg bone to extend, another set on the other side of the bone to retract the limb. This extra energy causes them to pull and tug against each other, producing trembling.

As blood is needed for this muscle-energizing process, your digestion stops. Digestion, you see, requires blood—and the blood is needed elsewhere. The stopping of your digestion manifests itself in the sinking sensation in your stomach: in butterflies. It also causes your mouth to go dry because salivating is a part of the digestive process.

Blushing is caused when the blood rapidly rushes through the capillaries to carry energy to where it is needed. Sweating relieves the body of weight and waste products, streamlining it for running or fighting; sweating also makes the skin slick and harder for a predator to grasp firmly.

With all this going on, it is pretty hard to talk well. The air is rushing up and down in the throat so rapidly that it is hard to control and to release as words and syllables. Also, the larynx, or voice box, is governed by the same kind of antagonistic muscle pairs, and these muscles are overenergized, too, so they are difficult to control. And there's the problem of the mind's going blank anyway, so that thinking up appropriate language is nearly impossible.

Why are talking and thinking thus a victim of this powerful emotion, fear? Well, in the case of our primordial caveman example, talking and thinking are completely irrelevant. In fact, talking and/or thinking could be quite counterproductive. If our caveman begins to talk to the tiger, what happens? He gets devoured! If he puts his cerebral cortex into high gear and begins to, say, compose a poem or a tract on the philosophical implications of meeting a sabre-toothed tiger on the path, does he survive? Hardly. He becomes the tiger's lunch. For our ancestors, from whom we have inherited our genes, thinking and talking came quite late in development—after the ability to survive physically became assured. Mother Nature did not consider talking and thinking very important for survival.

Speech, after all, is what we call an *overlaid function* of the so-called speech mechanism. Each feature of this speech mechanism has a much more primary function than that of producing speech.

Our lungs are inside our bodies not primarily to provide wind for our voices, but for breathing. We can live without talking. But without breathing? The nose and related cavities are also primarily for breathing—not for giving the voice timbre. The lips, tongue, teeth, palates, and so on are primarily for eating, not chopping sound up into words and syllables. Again, we can live without talking, but not without eating. Even the larynx, the voice box, is not primarily inside us to vibrate and thus provide sound for talking; it is there to keep foreign particles out of our otherwise defenseless lungs. For the purpose of talking, it is no better designed and developed than that of a healthy dog or cat.

To sum up, we can say that the chills, shakes, and gasps of fear in the presence of physical danger are normal, necessary, even vital for survival. Can you imagine a person who felt absolutely *no* fear in the face of physical danger? That person would be considered pretty strange by most people and would probably not live very long. In fact, even if we lower our inhibitions (that is, our ability to recognize and fear danger) artificially, with drugs or alcohol, we endanger ourselves. When intoxicated, we may not fear heights, or driving a hundred miles an hour, or proclaiming that we can lick anyone in the bar. We have blunted our ability to recognize and react protectively to danger.

So you say, OK, I see why I get all hyped up to cope with *physical* danger. But why do I react as if faced with death or dismemberment when all I am really faced with is standing up in front of people and talking?

There's an old educational film that asks that question. In it a fellow is talked into giving a speech about his Alaskan vacation, and right away he can't eat, sleep, work, or read that paper without being interrupted with the terrors. Of *what* is he scared, the announcer asks? Subsequent scenes then show our speaker falling off the platform, being attacked on the podium by a huge snake, and being shot with a huge pistol by a hostile audience member. No, the announcer says, he is *not* afraid of those events. But what scares him?

Danger. Not physical danger, but danger nonetheless. Psychological danger. And danger no less real or important because it is psychological rather than physical.

We human beings have left behind us the natural life to which we were once so well adapted—that of hunting and of gathering of food to sustain us. We now live in artificial societies governed by symbols; we have developed a set of abstract words and sounds that allows us to monkey around with concepts, notions, ideas. This kind of living paints on each of us a thin veneer of what we call *civilizing,* and it complicates our behavior far beyond that of our primordial ancestors. Each of us modern *Homo sapiens* must establish and maintain various self-images.

For instance, each of us has an intellectual self-image. Each of us regards himself or herself as pretty smart. And we want our fellows, especially our peers, to think of us as pretty smart. Well, public speaking is an intellectual endeavor. So, when you get up to give a speech, you expose your intellectual self-image to danger. Recognition of this danger to your intellectual image brings on your stage fright. You do not want people to walk away from the speech saying, "That stupid ignoramus," do you? No. You want them to walk away thinking, "My, what a brilliant speaker; if only I could do that so well."

We all have a social self-image. We like to think of ourselves as being highly likable, right? Well, speaking is a social process also. When you speak in public, you expose your social self-image. You want people to *like* you better as a result of your speech. But what are you scared of? You are afraid that some of the words in your *private* vocabulary—those perhaps reserved for good friends and not for mixed company—might slip out during your speech and ruin you. We all have repressed anger and aggression, dark thoughts kept to ourselves. We fear that one of these might reach consciousness and become exposed during our speech, revealing the black spots on our souls.

We all have a sexual self-image. Men wear their hair shorter (usually) and in a different style than do women. Men's clothes are designed differently from women's styles. Men wear, on the average, less makeup than do women. And in terms of emotions, women and men are supposed to fulfill different roles.

In our culture, men are supposed to model themselves after the heroes of that culture: Matt Dillon, Batman, Superman. The American male is supposed to be brave, fearless, courageous, and valiant, and *not* a scaredy-cat, yellow, and cowardly—not a sissy. Women, on the other hand, are supposedly the weaker sex; not only are they allowed to show all kinds of emotions publicly that men aren't, but women are supposed to be scared of mice and sounds in the dark. Women can show fear, in short, whereas men are not allowed to. That is why, in experiment after experiment, men will admit on questionnaires to less stage fright than will women, but they *demonstrate* more than do women. Not only are the men fearful of the danger to their other self-images when they speak, but they are afraid of being perceived by their audience as being afraid—and thus "unmanly."

One of my most severe stage-fright victims was a 200-pound football player. Stage fright nearly incapacitated him. For one assignment, I tape-recorded all the speeches of my students and played them back. My football player reacted with severe emotion to his playback. Afterward he asked me, "Do I *really* sound like that?" I assured him that he did. He smiled and straightened. "I always thought I had a high-pitched *feminine*-type voice," he said, "but on that tape I sound like a regular baritone. I talk like a *man!*" Most of his stage fright disappeared that day. Speaking no longer threatened his sexual self-image.

Eventually we all develop a self-image related to our job or profession. I have a professional self-image that can become threatened. I tell my classes that speaking before them does not make me nervous, but when I go to a convention of my academic peers from around the nation and the world and present a paper based on my professional research, I get just as nervous as any beginning orator. You will remember the incident, noted earlier in this chapter, concerning two speech professors who fainted during such presentations in New York in 1969. No doubt it was the perceived danger to their professional self-images that put them out.

Other self-images can be matters of concern that produce fear. Some people have a distorted cosmetic self-image; they think they *look* so bad that standing up in front of a group is painful. Most people have an economic self-image that can become endangered. Speaking to students may not bother me, but I am more apprehensive when I speak to the university's deans, vice-presidents, or president. These people have some control over my paycheck! And so it goes.

Knowing what effect an audience is going to have on which particular self-image(s) provides a true understanding of just why stage fright occurs. Several years ago the eminent British actor Sir Cedric Hardwicke was interviewed by a newspaper reporter.

"I suppose," said the reporter, "that after forty-six years on the stage, opening night jitters are a thing of the past for you?" Sir Cedric's reply, something of a shock, was "You know, it gets *worse* every year." This statement is perfectly understandable. Each year on the stage heightens the actor's reputation and "self-image." She or he has more to lose each year, therefore, by forgetting lines on opening night. If the young ingenue makes a serious mistake onstage, that's OK—it's to be expected. But Sir Cedric Hardwicke making such a gaffe would flash across the theatrical headlines of the world!

Let's pause and make a most important point now. Earlier I said that the fear reaction to physical danger was normal, natural, and even vital for survival. Can the same be said of the fear reaction to "psychological" danger? Is the stage fright experienced when one's self-images are in danger *real*? Is it normal? Natural? Vital for survival?

You bet it is.

Given the kind of culture we live in, rich in symbolic interactions with our fellows and complicated by highly intricate social, legal, and political interrelationships, being scared to give a public speech is as normal as eating when you are hungry. In fact, if giving a speech to a valued group of people does *not* make you nervous, you should begin to doubt your sanity. To improve on Kipling, "If you can keep your head when all about you are losing theirs, perhaps you don't understand the seriousness of the situation."

Can you imagine a person with not a care in the world about self-images? What would you call a guy who didn't give a farthing what people thought of him intellectually, socially, professionally, cosmetically, economically, and so on? How about "crackpot"? "Outcast"? "Misanthrope"? "Screwball"? "Nut"?

The truth is that in this artificial, civilized world in which we live, it is quite necessary to develop, maintain, and protect a number of various self-images. And it thus becomes quite normal, necessary, and vital to survival to recognize a threat to any of these self-images and to react biologically as if we were in serious physical danger. And, again, if our "normal" capacity to react with fear to a self-image threat is artificially impaired by drugs or alcohol, we are apt to say and do things that will hurt us. Sober, we would restrain ourselves from angry or obscene words; drunk, we may say things to our friends, our bosses, or our spouses that would depreciate our social or economic standing. Under normal circumstances, we might perceive when our audience grows restless; doped up with tranquilizers, we might drone on until we anesthetize them.

OK, you agree, even stage fright is normal, natural, and vital to survival. So what can I do to overcome it?

Well, first of all, you will never *overcome* it, if by that you mean "no longer experience it." As long as you are alive and remain "normal" psychologically, you will always experience some stage fright when a self-image is threatened by a speaking engagement. There is no way to get around that fact. But you can diminish it to the point where you can handle it. As one woman put it, after completing a course in public speaking, "I still have the butterflies when I speak, but now they fly in formation."

If you have followed my reasoning thus far, you have already taken the first step to lowering your stage fright level. You understand and believe that stage fright is normal, natural, and vital to survival. And you know that it is felt universally by all normal human beings. You need not "fear fear itself." Let me explain.

All too often this is what happens. A young man has to give a speech. When his name is called, he rises and approaches the podium. He is naturally nervous; after all, he is putting his various self-images on the line. His nervousness is natural, normal, and so on, but he does not think so. He is thinking, "These classmates (or whatever) are going to see me shake and sweat. They are going to realize that I am scared. They will see that I am unlike Matt Dillon, Superman, Batman. They will have words for me: *coward, yellow, scaredy-cat, sissy.*" This prospect of being perceived as afraid now makes things worse; the mind goes even blanker, the sweat pours even more profusely, and the shakes multiply in ferocity. "My gosh," the tyro speaker says to himself, "it's getting worse instead of better. They're going to see how spineless and how faint-hearted I am." This latest perception becomes the impetus for even further and more heightened fear reactions, which might produce more heightened perceptions of threat, which can lead to even more diligent fear reactions, on and on in a spiral of self-acceleration.

But with the right set of attitudes and beliefs about fear, our novice speaker reacts differently. Called on to speak, he strides to the lectern. He recognizes his fear reactions as normal. He says to himself, "Lucky me. I'm normal. I am a little nervous, but that will only give me the extra energy I need to be dynamic in this speech. The audience will notice I'm a little shaky, but they know it's normal too, and they won't care. Besides, a minute or so into the speech I'll be quite calmed down from this initial anxiety." In other words, our speaker, with the proper attitude, refuses to be sucked into the spiral of self-accelerating threat/fear reaction/increased threat/increased fear reaction/increased threat cycle. In short, he has learned to not fear fear itself. Get the picture?

Besides your attitude toward fear itself, another set of attitudes is of prime importance in reducing stage fright: your attitudes toward yourself. The key is to *understand* yourself and then to *accept* yourself as you are or can be. In other words, your perceptions of your self-images should be *accurate* perceptions; then those self-images are the ones you should decide to live with in peace. As Bonaro Overstreet wrote in *Understanding Fear in Ourselves and Others,* "Perhaps the most important thing we can undertake toward the reduction of fear is to make it easier for people to accept themselves; to like themselves."

There are several specific things you can also do to minimize your initial stage fright reactions and symptoms. Doing these things is based on your understanding of the causes of your problem.

Reducing the Size of the Threat

The amount of fear reaction you experience will be directly proportional to the size of the threat. *Size of threat = amount of fear reaction* is as much an equation as $2 \times 2 = 4$. And the point about mathematical equations you learned back in grade school is that when you reduce one side of the equation, the other side must be reduced. So if you reduce the size of the threat, you reduce the amount of fear symptoms you would otherwise feel. How do you reduce the size of the threat? There are three ways.

✓First, speak on a topic that you know well, a topic that you have spoken about to others, that you have studied for a particular reason, that you have an interest in. For instance, I feel pretty comfortable speaking to groups about any one of several topics in the area of communication; I can discuss the psychology of humor (my research specialty) easily before groups; or I can comfortably speak on several aspects of photography (being an amateur photographer). But I would be scared out of my wits to try to give a speech on atomic physics to the American Physical Society.

Second, be prepared. Most stage fright is really "lack-of-preparation" fright. It is fear of failure, because the speaker knows that the work that would ensure success has not been done. Are you a student? If so I'll bet there have been times when you went to an examination for which you were not really prepared. You had not taken the time to read and re-read the text thoroughly; you had not done some of the outside readings; or you had not been able to outline, type, and study your notes sufficiently. Perhaps you had missed several class periods when important material was discussed. Well, I'm sure you went into that exam with less than full confidence!

However, I hope that you have also had the experience at least once or twice of going to an examination well prepared. What a difference. You were never absent; you took excellent notes, reworking them into a rational whole, and then typing them up and studying them thoroughly. You read your text material, outlined it, reread it over and over, picking out key points to memorize, and so on. In such circumstances, you can go to your exam with dry palms and a placid cardiovascular system because you feel that no question your instructor can ask will stump you!

The same is true of speaking. If you have faithfully followed the advice and preparatory steps outlined in Chapter 2, if you have worked diligently to find interesting and varied materials for your speech, have rehearsed and honed it before a live audience several times, and, as a result, feel that you have a really important message for your audience that you can get across to them with authority and clarity, your chances for failure dramatically diminish. And so will your stage fright.

If, on the other hand, you wait until the eleventh hour to begin work on your speech and have to throw it together in a panic, you have every right to expect a terrific case of the jitters as your speaking occasion approaches. Remember, it is by hard work that you even earn the right to be speaking.

A third way to reduce the size of the threat of speaking is simply to be in as good physical condition as possible. Get a good night's sleep the night before your speech. Eat nutritious food, and avoid any food or drink that will upset your nervous or gastrointestinal system. Of course, if you wait until the eleventh hour to work on your speech, this may not be possible. A student of mine, giving his final speech, produced a complete disaster. He was so nervous he could not remember what he wanted to say. He stumbled around as if he were punch-drunk. One eye was so red it looked as if he had scratched out the white with a fingernail. Later he came to tell me he could not understand why he had done such a punk job on the speech. "Honest," he said, "I worked on it all night; I didn't even go to bed!"

Countering Physiological Reactions

Your problem is that your autonomic nervous system has prepared your body for a physical danger that you must either fight or run from. But you are going to give a speech, not fight or run. So you have more strength and energy than you need. Solution? Get rid of some of the excess. How? There are three ways.

First, before you even get up to speak, alternately tense up and then relax your muscles. Crunch your toes down into the floor and feel how much energy your leg muscles burn up. Then relax them and feel the tension drain away. Do the same with the muscles of your arms and your chest. Do some isometrics. Place your palms together before your chest or stomach (maybe even down under the desk or table, unseen), and press your hands together vigorously. Then relax them. Lots of energy has been used up. Grip the sides of your chair seat and try to lift yourself straight up; then relax. If you are to be introduced while "off-stage" and then are going to walk on, you can practice lifting the piano, or do some deep-knee bends while awaiting your entrance cue (I did the latter in the minister's office moments before walking out to the sanctuary to get married).

You can also use up some of that excess energy while you are speaking, through gestures, directed movement, shrugs of the shoulders, changing facial expression—in short, through being a "loose," animated speaker.

Now, I know that the beginning speaker almost instinctively tries to stand as still during a speech as possible. You do this because you subconsciously realize that by moving and gesturing you will draw attention to yourself, and one of your instinctual behaviors, *running away*, includes the tendency to hide. But such behavior is totally antithetical to public speaking. You should want to be drawing attention to yourself! That's why you are standing up speaking while everyone else is sitting down listening. And if you stand there like a stick, moving only your mouth, crouching down as low as possible behind the lectern, not only will you look unnatural and artificial, you will not be using up that excess energy pumping through your body.

A third way to try to bring your bodily processes into a more comfortable homeostatic balance is to "catch up" on your need for oxygen. Many people report that taking several deep, deep breaths before rising to speak makes their breathing much more normal. However, try this a time or two at home before doing it right before your next speech; a few such deep breaths only make some people dizzy.

Replacing Emotion with Intellectual Activity

You will remember that the numbness in your cerebral cortex as your speech event draws near is the result of your lower brain's taking over and preparing the body for a physical and not a social or psychological danger. Mother Nature is decreeing that you must act, not think or talk. You must reverse this cycle.

It is a well-known principle in psychology that emotional activity can replace intellectual activity ("I couldn't help myself; I lost my *head!*"), but it is also clear that intellectual activity can replace emotional activity. For instance, if you are sitting and watching a scary movie, such as *The Exorcist* or *The Amityville Horror,* you are not likely to feel the hair rise at the nape of your neck if you are busily trying to figure out how the Hollywood technicians achieved the fantastic special effects you are witnessing.

This principle works in speaking. If you can get off to a good start in talking, which is an intellectual activity, the cerebral cortex will begin right away to retake command of your total organism. How can you ensure that you will get off to a good start in speaking? Begin with an introduction that is impossible to forget.

One type of introduction is absolutely unforgettable. Tell a story of something that happened to you that will illustrate your topic. How in the world can you forget such an introduction? It happened to you; you had direct, physical experience with these events; you have probably told the story before, perhaps even elaborating on it over the years. When I was a speech student years ago, I was to make a speech on the concept that "we learn and remember something much better if we know the cause or basic principle behind it." I began it this way:

> As a Boy Scout, I had to learn how to find my way out of the woods if lost, without a compass, and when the sun was obscured by clouds. In other words, I had to know which side of a tree had the thickest moss. I would memorize "north" one day and the next day be asking myself, "Is it north, or is it south?" Then one day my patrol leader explained *why* it is north. Moss grows where it is darkest and dampest, and the north side of a tree gets less sunshine than the other sides. This taught me that . . .

By the time I got to my statement of purpose, my breathing and heartbeat were both back to nearly normal.

Another trick some speakers use is to begin a speech by reading some item. It might be a little poem, an item from a newspaper or a magazine, a clever quotation, or an anecdote. I am not advocating that you read your entire speech, but reading some short item by way of introducing your speech is quite legitimate. A young man in one of my classes gave a speech on the Equal Rights Amendment and the women's movement in general. He began by lifting a note card and reading:

> Women, it is now quite clear, are very much like men,
> Except, of course, for here and there, and sometimes now and then.

Another began a speech by saying that just that morning she had received a note in the mail, which she read:

I know that today you are giving that big speech, and I am sure you will do an outstanding job of it. With your superior intelligence, quick wit, indomitable personality, and your deep and profound insight into the human heart, you will deliver a masterpiece of oratory.

Love,
Mother

You can increase intellectual activity by having a *speech* that is hard to forget, too. To do this, you need to use as many mnemonic (memory) devices as possible, such as good organization. It is a psychological truism that organized material is easier to remember than unorganized material. More will be said about this in Chapter 5.

Phrasing the purpose of your speech in easily remembered words will also help (and help your *audience* to remember your speech). For instance, one of my speech students, extremely able scholastically, gave a speech on his formula for maintaining an almost perfect A average. His four major points were read, reflect, recite, then review.

Countering Emotion with Emotion

We often express our ambivalence about something by saying that we have "mixed emotions." What are mixed emotions?

Psychology tells us that we cannot feel two quite different emotions at the same time. We can feel the two emotions by alternating them very quickly; this is what we really mean by mixed emotions. But just try feeling sorry for yourself at the same time that you are laughing at yourself. It can't be done.

So replace fear with some other emotion as you begin your speech. Many people begin a speech with a little humorous anecdote that gently pokes fun at themselves. The speaker who began with the note from "Mother" did so, with great effect. It is pretty hard to be taking yourself very seriously if you are joking at yourself.

You might also begin your speech with a kind of righteous indignation over the topic of your speech. "Here is a problem that *must* be solved," you repeat to yourself over and over.

Become audience-centered. Develop a real concern that your

audience will understand and perhaps even act on your message. It's pretty hard to be self-centered (which is what stage fright is all about, anyway) if you are centering all your energy and attention on your audience.

Assignment Versus Message

In case you are reading this book as part of an academic course in speaking, let us reconsider a point made in Chapter 1.

If you approach each speech merely as an assignment, it is likely that your stage fright will be unnecessarily high. If, however, you can approach each assignment as a genuine opportunity to communicate worthwhile information and ideas to a group of people you like and admire, if you feel that you truly have worthwhile goods to deliver, your stage fright will diminish. You will work hard, look forward to stepping in front of the class, and do a good job. You will feel that you have done your audience a genuine favor by sharing yourself with them, and you will *not* feel the necessity of concluding your speech with that old bromide, "Thank you." Furthermore, when you finish, you will feel that you have had fun, and you will be pleased with yourself.

4

Raise the Ante— and the Stakes

T he single most important aspect of your speech will be your content—what you will say when you stand up to speak. That content has to come from somewhere. Where and how do you go about finding it?

If You Are an Expert

Are you already an expert who will be speaking on your area of expertise? Then finding your material should be easy. Much of it, of course, should already be in your head. The rest may be within arm's length.

Are you the best beekeeper in the county? Then your bookshelves probably bulge with beekeeping books and pamphlets and magazines you have collected and already read. Maybe you have even written some of that stuff. Are you an urban social worker who must deal with drunks and dope users regularly? Then you probably have a wealth of personal knowledge and own an abundance of printed material on alcoholism and drug abuse. Are you a thoracic surgeon? Then you already have a copious amount of knowledge plus numerous volumes on defects of the human heart, lungs, and liver. Is your principal avocation an active opposition to the proliferation of nuclear power plants? Then you probably have reams of material supporting the antinuke position.

For the expert, developing the speech does not mean that much material will have to be found. The expert's principal problems are to decide what to leave out of the speech and to decide how to organize what's left into a meaningful pattern.

If You Are Not an Expert

If you are not an expert, you don't have a lot of specialized knowledge of a topic either in your head or lying about your living quarters. You need to find that specialized knowledge (and, even a real expert might have to go dig up some extra information). That usually means going to the library.

There are other sources of information, of course. For instance, I always recommend to my students that they keep up with what is going on in the world. I tell them they should read, thoroughly, at least one good daily newspaper; that they should read thoroughly at least one good weekly newsmagazine, such as *Time, Newsweek,* or *U.S. News and World Report;* and that they should keep up with the world, national, and local news via radio and television. Such keeping up, I tell them, could save them some embarrassment. For instance, I once sat through a student speech that argued vociferously that marriages between blacks and Caucasians should be made illegal through the passing of state laws. The young woman speaking was oblivious to the fact that, two years before, the Supreme Court had ruled such laws unconstitutional.

You can always go to a newsstand or bookstore for information. Or there may be an expert on your topic nearby whom you could interview and, perhaps, borrow printed information from. You could invest in a long-distance telephone call in order to interview a more distant expert. If you work for a large commercial, governmental, or educational organization, you might find that you have access to that organization's considerable research-and-development department.

But getting material for a speech usually means going to the library.

If you are going to be a speaker, then you have to learn to find in the library, in the most efficient way possible, the information you need (unless you can afford to hire someone to do it for you). This means you need to find out systematically what your library holds and how to find it.

I can hardly tell you how to use the particular library available to you. Many libraries conduct tours for new users; some even provide self-guided tours via audio-cassette recorders. You need to inquire how to find your way around your own storehouse of knowledge and wisdom.

To give you some idea of what to look for, and how to go looking, let me describe my own little library exercise, which I trot my students through at the University of Georgia. Remember, now, all the details of this exercise pertain in particular just to the library at the University of Georgia, which is an excellent research library, but this exercise should be adaptable, at least in part, to almost any good library.

Early in the quarter, I pass out to my students a single mimeographed page. It asks them to perform specific tasks.

Their first series of tasks involves finding the reference room. At the University of Georgia, it is on the first floor; the main reference room is generally in a very prominent place in any other library, too, and is usually quite large.

The student is directed to the reference tables where the *Readers' Guide to Periodical Literature* is to be found. The student is to find five periodicals indexed in the guide that begin with the letter "S" and to write their titles in the spaces provided.

The *Readers' Guide* is an excellent index to articles in hundreds of periodical publications from *Aging* through *Mechanix Illustrated* to *The Yale Review*. The articles are indexed alphabetically by subject matter and provide all the bibliographical information necessary to finding a particular article. Part of a sample page of the guide is reproduced below*:

226   READERS' GUIDE TO PERIODICAL LITERATURE

HUMAN figure in art
Attack of inspiration [A. Siani's suit against painter P. Georges' portrayal in work entitled The mugging of the muse] Vasari. il Art News 80:9+ Ap '81
Can a figurative work of art be libelous? [pro and con discussion of A. Siani-J. Silberman suit against P. Georges' portrayal in work entitled The mugging of the muse] R. Longman. il Am Artist 45:16-17+ Ap '81
Drawing the human figure: an interview with Burt Silverman [interview by P. Van Gelder] B. Silverman. il Am Artist 45:62-7 Jl '81
Movement and self-concept: children's figure drawings. D. M. Pruett. bibl il Des Arts Educ 82:36-9 My/Je '81
Soft sculptures by Michele Brower. A. Meister. il por Am Artist 45:64-9+ My '81

                 Exhibitions
Clay figure [exhibition at American Craft Museum. New York City] D. Bourdon. il Vogue 171:40+ My '81
Perceiving the clay figure [exhibition at the American Craft Museum. N.Y.] D. Ashton. il Am Craft 41:24-31 Ap/My '81
HUMAN hair as deer repellent. See Deer baits and repellents
HUMAN locomotion
    See also
    Running
HUMAN mechanics
Letters from Emile Jaques-Dalcroze: the singular joy of scrutinizing Stravinsky [ed by R. Craft] E. Jaques-Dalcroze. il por Dance Mag 55:80-2+ Ap '81
HUMAN powered vehicles. See Manpowered vehicles
HUMAN relations
    See also
    Helping behavior
    Lesbianism
    Monogamy
    Polygamy
    Prejudice
    Revenge

HUMIDITY
    See also
    Hot weather
Oxygen isotope ratios in trees reflect mean annual temperature and humidity. R. L. Burk and M. Stuiver. bibl f il Science 211:1417-19 Mr 26 '81
HUMMA, John
Mother. 71; Berchie. 93 [poem] Commonweal 108: 342 Je 5 '81
HUMMEL, Berta
Berta Hummel and her figurines. F. A. Burrows. il Hobbies 86:32-3 Jl '81 *
HUMOR
Wit and the emancipators [address. April 16, 1981] R. L. Birch. Vital Speeches 47:536-8 Je 15 '81
                 Bibliography
Some are very mice indeed [children's jokes, riddles, games and puns] R. Lasson. N Y Times Bk R 86:51+ Ap 26 '81
HUMOR, Chinese
Crosstalk [tr by C. Rosen] B. L. Hou. il Sierra 66:12-13 Mr/Ap '81
HUMOR in motion pictures
    See also
    Motion pictures—Comedy films
HUMORISTS
    See also
    Perelman, Sidney Joseph
HUMPBACK whales. See Whales
HUMUS
Sludge decomposition and stabilization. R. Hartenstein. bibl f il Science 212:743-9 My 15 '81
HUNGARIANS in Canada
Enduring vein of courage [memoirs of former Hungarian political prisoner G. Gabori] B. Amiel. il por Macleans 94:40 Je 29 '81
HUNGARY
    See also
    Political prisoners—Hungary

*Partial page reproduced here by permission of *Readers' Guide to Periodical Literature*.

To some readers of this book, this information presented on *Readers' Guide* may seem utterly elementary. But you would be astounded to know how many college students, even juniors and seniors, I have found in four different universities who are entirely ignorant of the existence of the guide.

The student next is asked to find a work by call number (Ref/Z1002/B5685 at the University of Georgia) and write down how many volumes there are. The work is the five-volume *World Bibliography of Bibliographies,* supplemented by a sixth volume to update the other five. Having once done this, the student should be able to find the title of virtually any bibliography published anywhere on any topic.

Back at the reference tables, the student must locate the *Education Index* and find in it the bibliographical information on at least three articles published since 1976 dealing with the use of television in teaching. This bibliographical information is written onto the worksheet. The student should now know how to find articles published in both popular magazines and professional and technical journals on any subject relevant to education, whether it be the effects of busing on integration, the value and use of grades, college honor systems, or the criteria for hiring and firing schoolteachers or professors.

Having found and used this one, specialized subject-matter index, the student is now required to find three other special-subject indexes, one of which ought to be an index of the subject matter in which the student is or will be majoring. She or he can prowl the reference tables to find them, ask the reference library staff, or consult the card catalog or computerized printout of periodicals and the index of that printout. Some of the specialized indexes found include *The Index to Journals in Communication, Psychological Abstracts, Sociological Abstracts, Applied-Science and Technology Index, Engineering Index, Index to Legal Periodicals, Industrial Arts Index, Social Sciences and Humanities Index, Biological and Agricultural Index,* and *Public Affairs Information Service.* Knowing of these, the student should be able to find specialized information on almost any subject.

The student next must find the *subject* card catalog, locate three books on the subject of "Sharks," and write down their titles. This portion of the card catalog lists all the books and other publications in the library alphabetically by subject matter. Then the student is directed to find the author and title portion of the card catalog and to find the call number of the book *Die Laughing,* by Richard Lockridge. The student now knows how to use the real key to the library, the card catalog; he or she can find published material on a topic even without knowing the author or title of the work; if the author or title is known, the work can be found more swiftly in the author and title section.

Next I have the student go to the reference desk, ask for a particular volume by call number, which at the University of Georgia is REF/HG/4057/p.7/ 19— (current year)/v. 1, and write down the title. This tome, published annually, is *Standard and Poor's Register of Corporations, Directors, and Executives* (usually shortened to *Standard and Poor's*). It lists much information about every corporation in America, including the names of its officers and the way to contact any officer or corporation. The student is directed specifically to find and record the name of the president of Fisher-Price Toys and the name of the company that owns Fisher-Price Toys (Quaker Oats). The student now knows how to contact any officer of any corporation providing any service or manufacturing any product in the country; through these contacts, the student can seek information or make complaints about the company. Knowing specifically whom to contact enhances a reply.

Most of our students do not know that our library, like many libraries, contains a large collection of big-city telephone directories. To impress this holding on my students, I have them find our collection in the reference room and locate and record the home address of Maxine M. Trauernicht of Lincoln, Nebraska. Now the student should be able to locate a variety of information on a number of cities and to dial direct anyone in one of those cities to obtain specific information.

Suppose a student wants some information on which colleges are on the semester system and which on the quarter or trimester system? Or what colleges do and do not have honor systems or coed dormitories or student cooperatives? To acquaint my students with the fact that our library has a very large collection of college catalogs, I direct them to that section of the reference room to find the date of registration for the next summer term of the New School for Social Research in New York.

To demonstrate to students that the history of a word can be found easily, I direct them to find out how many volumes there are of a massive, scholarly etymological dictionary called *The Oxford English Dictionary* (call number: Folio/PE/1625/.M7/1933 at the University of Georgia). They are to look up the word *humor;* specifically, they are to find meaning number II4 listed there and write down the date (1475) when the word is first known to have been published with that meaning.

As you might imagine, the student by now has put in some mileage in the reference room and should know how to get around it and obtain a wealth of information, along with specific references to a veritable cornucopia of more information.

The student now is sent to our library basement, where a number of things are kept, mostly our microfilm collection and current and bound periodical literature. Current newspapers from all over the United States and the world are also available.

The student is supposed to learn here how to find "all the news that's fit to print," in the current and back issues of *The New York Times,* on microfilm. The student must find in *The New York Times Index* three recent articles on Reggie Jackson and write down the bibliographical data. This index, like the *Readers' Guide,* lists articles in the *Times* by subject matter, alphabetically. A part of a page from the index is reproduced below by permission of *The New York Times:*

REDFORD, Robert. See also Motion Pictures—Awards, D 20
REDUCING Pills and Devices. Use Weight
REED, Everett C. See also Albany International Corp, D 18
REED, Robert (Suspect). See also Murders—NYS, Blair, Annie, D 24
REEVE, Christopher. See also Jaycees, D 19
REFORESTATION. Use Forests
REFORM and Reorganization (Institutional). See also Children—Med, D 19. Courts—US, D 29. Crime—US, D 20. Firearms, D 22,30. Fires--NYC, D 26. Housing—US, D 27. Immigration—US, D 28. Indians, D 19. Intl Rel—US, D 16,24,30. Jury System, D 29. Labor—US—Discrimination, D 31. Labor—US—Indus Hazards, D 16. NYC—Pol, D 27. New York New Haven & Hartford RR Co, D 16. NYS—Finances—Budget, D 21. Pregnancy, D 19,21. Pres Elections, D 18,27,31. Pres Elections—Electoral College, D 19. RRs—US—Passenger, D 21,28. Salvador, El, D 18,19. Social Security (US), D 22,27. Supreme Court (US), D 29. Taxation—Conn, D 21. US—Econ Conditions, D 24, 30. US—Finances—Budget, D 30. US—Finances—Fed Revenue Sharing, D 22,27. US—Law and Legis (Fed)—Filibusters and Debate Curbs, D 28. US—Pol—Dem Party, D 21. US—Pol—Transition Between Administrations, D 19. US—Population—Census, D 31. US Armament—General Policy and Strategy, D 24. Welfare (US), D 22,27. Welfare (US)—Conn, D 28. Welfare (US)—NYS, D 20,31. Other geog headings, subdivided Departments and Agencies where subdivided
REFORM Judaism (Headings). See headings beginning Jewish or Judaism
REFORMATORIES. Use Prisons
REFRIGERATION Equipment. See also Air Conditioning
REFUGEES and Expatriates. Note: For pol refugees, see geog headings denoting refugees' origin. For war

Finally, the student must find the microfilm copy of *The New York Times* published on his or her birth date and record three headlines of other events that occurred that day. Now the student can find and read on a microfilm reader any issue of *The New York Times* and of any of a large number of newspapers and magazines.

I next have the student go up to the second floor. This is where we keep our large collection of government documents. The student is to find who publishes the *Monthly Catalogue of U.S. Government Publications* and write the title in the report. Then the student is to ask one of the librarians on that floor what kind of assistance those librarians can provide for students.

We have an unusual room on the third floor of our library called "The Georgia Room." It contains works by Georgians and about Georgia and Georgians, including the telephone directory for every city, town, village, and crossroads in the state. I have the student go there to find out what is there, to list one work to be found there, and to tell why it is there.

Finally, I have the student find the bound journal with the call number PN4071/S8. This is a professional journal of my field, *Communication Monographs* (formerly *Speech Monographs*), which contains reports of original research in my field. The student is to photocopy one page from an issue dated 1975 or later and turn it in with the library report. The student is also required to find at least one professional journal in the student's own or proposed major field that publishes reports of original research, and to write down its title. Some of the titles turned in are *Public Opinion Quarterly, Journal of Broadcasting, Journalism Quarterly, Bulletin of the Atomic Scientists, Business Quarterly, Forest Science, Horticultural Research, Legislative Review, Music Review, Poultry Digest,* and *The Pharmaceutical Journal.*

Once a student has completed and turned in this library exercise I assume that I have proof positive that that student will never fail to have prepared a speech because of the excuse, "I couldn't find any information on my topic"! Likewise, if you will take some sort of tour of your library like the one described here, you also will forever be without the same excuse.

After you have found where to look for material to put into your speech, what kind of material do you look for? Of course, much of your speech material will be *you:* your ideas, your generalizations, your knowledge based on experience, and so on. But what kind of material do you want to find through interviews, phone calls, or the library? Most of what you will be looking for is *supporting* material, specific material that will *support* (or help to explain or prove) the ideas you are trying to put across to your audience. Let us consider the several kinds of supporting material: facts and figures, examples, comparison and contrast, testimony, repetition and restatement, definition, description, wit and humor, and visual aids.

Supporting Material

Facts and Figures. What is a "fact"? Something that is "true"? Not exactly. As Edward Bunker once stated, "Facts and truth are often cousins—not brothers." "Truth" can be instinctual or spiritual. A fact is something that is actual, either an entity or an occurrence. We say that a man is an "accessory after the fact," meaning that he became an accessory after the actual commission of a crime. A statement of a fact is a statement about an occurrence or an entity, and that statement may or not be true or correct. To say that the earth is spherical is to make a more-or-less correct statement of fact; to say that the moon is made of green cheese is to make a statement of fact that our astronauts have shown to be incorrect.

Statements of fact used in speeches should be as correct as you can determine and as specific as possible. In a speech, you should not use ambiguities such as "several years ago." Be specific and factual: "in June of 1976."

Figures are usually statements of fact employing specific quantities. Again, your figures should be as specific as possible and as correct as possible. Instead of "Our trip was really long, and we burned a lot of gasoline," say, "We drove 5,324 miles on our trip and used 252 gallons of gasoline." Bernard Baruch once said that "Every man has a right to his opinion, but no man has a right to be wrong in his facts."

Good speeches are usually liberally peppered with specific facts and figures. Such use of factual material is convincing to your audience, and their use is likely to make your audience think, "Wow, this speaker has really done some homework and certainly seems to know the subject!"

On March 29, 1979, Mr. Fred L. Hartley, President of Union Oil Company of California, made a speech entitled "The Surge in Energy and Construction Labor Costs" to the National Association of Manufacturers in Washington. Read how he creatively wove facts and figures together to make his point:

> As late as October 1973, Saudi Arabian light crude, the marker oil from which all quantities are scaled, was sold to all comers at $2.32 a barrel. In 1974, the price was $10.84, up 400 percent. Even without the Iranian upheaval, the price in October of this year would have been at least $14.54, or 625 percent higher than the price at the beginning of the 1973 embargo. The $3.70 price increase since 1974 is attributable to nothing but U.S. inflation and deterioration of the dollar.
>
> To put all this in perspective, when I came with Union Oil 40 years ago on May 18, 1939, a dollar contained 10 dimes and had the construction purchasing power of 10 dimes. Today, it has the purchasing power of one 1939 dime. In 1939, domestic crude oil was typically $1.25 to $1.50 per barrel at the refinery gate. Multiply by 10 and you get about the 1978 delivered world price of $14.00 per barrel. This contrasts with the U.S. regulated domestic composite price of $9.30 per barrel.[1]

Mr. Hartley's reference to the dollar's purchasing power in terms of 1939 dimes indicates that he had followed the maxim of John Burroughs: "To treat your facts with imagination is one thing, but to imagine your facts is another."

Hartley reemphasized the effect of inflation on our shrinking dollars later in his speech:

> The realities of these statistics were driven home to my company in Alaska last year when we completed a twin to a chemical fertilizer plant that was constructed in 1969. It cost us more than three times as much as the original unit and yet it was developed essentially from similar blueprints. And this tripling of cost occurred over a period of only nine years.[2]

---

[1] Fred L. Hartley, "The Surge in Energy and Construction Labor Costs," *Vital Speeches of the Day*, June 1, 1979, p. 488. Quoted by permission of *Vital Speeches of the Day*.

[2] *Ibid.*, p. 489. Quoted by permission of *Vital Speeches of the Day*.

Hartley's combining of numerical data here is what we call the use of *statistics*, of course, and we must remember Benjamin Disraeli's plaint: "There are three kinds of lies; lies, damned lies, and statistics." The truth of the matter is that, of course, it is easy to lie with statistics. Most people will gullibly swallow any "factual" material if it is presented in statistical form because it sounds so *scientific*. "The ad said, '23 percent more cures,' Honey, *not* 22 percent or 24 percent; that study must have been *accurate*."

Bosh. Before accepting statistics as "truth," do a little poking. To come up with a statistic, someone must have counted something in some way. Find out who did the counting and how it was done. Suppose I told you I did a poll here at the campus and found that two thirds of the students polled thought that the U.S. income tax rate should be doubled. You would probably ask me whom I polled, right? I reply, "I asked the first three people who walked out of the foreign student office, and two of the three said they favored the idea." Remember, statistics are very much like a bikini; what they reveal is suggestive, but what they conceal is vital.

Examples.   Have you ever sat there listening to a speech or lecture on some complex and abstract phenomenon, your brow knit in concentration as you tried to follow the ideas the speaker struggled to get across? And then the speaker said something like "Let me give you an example. Just three years ago right here in this very town . . ." Ah! Then did you sit back, smile, unknit your brow, nod your head, and think, "Oh. Now I see"? As columnist Jenkin Lloyd Jones had said,

> Skilled speakers go easy on abstractions and heavy on specific example. Unless an audience is constantly dragged back to a world it knows and understands it will drift off. Jesus understood the power of parable, and Abe Lincoln often made a political point leap to life by beginning: 'There was an old farmer down in Sangamon County . . .'[3]

I like to distinguish between two kinds of examples: illustrations and specific instances. Illustrations are longer, narrative

---

[3] Jenkin Lloyd Jones, "Short Course in Public Speaking," *Greenville* (NC) *News*, November 28, 1970. Quoted by permission of Mr. Jones.

examples; specific instances are brief examples that are either self-explanatory or instantly recognizable as examples.

In his speech "Is the Free Press in America Under Attack?" Walter Cronkite of CBS made the point that our freedom of the press *is* under attack and visualized what would happen if that freedom were lost. He exemplified the consequences with an illustration:

> You know, there was an experience shared by many of us who were in Germany at the end of the Second World War that I think is sharply relevant to this issue. People would come up to us, and with tears in their eyes they would tell us that they had no idea of the horrors of Auschwitz and Buchenwald . . . they just didn't know. The curious thing was that many of them were telling the truth, or a half-truth anyway. Most probably they didn't know the full horror or let themselves think about it if they suspected. After all, they had surrendered their civic eyes along with their national soul. They had helped to dismantle their own democracy and had made no complaint when freedom of the press was abolished. They weren't informed of the gas chambers; at least most weren't.[4]

This illustration is what we call a *literal* or a *factual illustration;* it describes what happened. Sometimes you can make your point just as well, or even better, by using a *hypothetical* illustration. A hypothetical illustration puts into concrete terms what might or could happen if such-and-such came to pass. In the same speech, Mr. Cronkite blasted a recent U.S. Supreme Court ruling that police could search and ransack a newspaper office for evidence with only a search warrant (not a subpoena, which is more difficult to come by). In his attack, Cronkite used two hypothetical illustrations:

> Think of what might have happened if this ruling had been in effect during the Nixon administration. For one thing, the Pentagon Papers might never have seen the light of day. The White House could easily have gotten a warrant from some federal judge and seized them, early on, from *The New York Times*.
>
> And what a field day the likes of Haldeman, Ehrlichman, Mitch-

---

[4]Walter Cronkite, "Is the Free Press in America Under Attack?" *Vital Speeches of the Day*, March 15, 1979, pp. 333–334. Quoted by permission of *Vital Speeches of the Day*.

ell, and Colson might have had if this decision had been in force at the time of the Watergate break-in. Who knows? With judiciously timed ransackings of the offices of *The Washington Post* and *The New York Times,* they might have uncovered enough sources and plugged enough leaks to contain that scandal sufficiently to save Richard Nixon's hold on the presidency.

Such scandals at the national level, fortunately, are rare. But they are less rare at the local level, and it is there that the impact of the "knock on the door decision," as it's been called, could be particularly devastating. A hypothetical example:

An honest minor official, or merely a disgruntled one working in a City Hall run by a corrupt political machine, begins feeding information to the local newspaper. The information touches on a kickback scheme which can be traced all the way to the top, if the leak isn't plugged. But it is. The machine's police chief, or the machine's D.A., with the flimsiest of excuses, goes to one of the *machine's* judges for a search warrant, and the paper is ransacked. While pawing through files and desk drawers, the searchers find the name of the newspaper's source on the kickback story. That honest official might be fired and threatened with prosecution on some trumped up charge if he did any more talking to the press. Or he might be intimidated in some other fashion. In some precincts, he might very well end up in the trunk of a car. In any case, the leak would be fixed. And the word would go out to other potential whistle-blowers that there is no way they can depend on remaining anonymous.[5]

Because the illustration, either factual or hypothetical, explains an issue in such a down-to-earth, realistic, flesh-and-blood manner, it is no wonder that so many speech experts consider it probably the most potent form of support with a general audience. Look for *good* illustrations for every one of your speeches. *Specific instances* are used in strings or bunches, one after another, to produce a cumulative effect in the minds of the audience. Consider this string of specific instances to back up the contention that "The freedom of the press has suffered serious setbacks in recent years":

In *Gannett vs. DePasquale,* the Supreme Court ruled that the press could be barred from a criminal courtroom.
In their *Zurcher vs. Stanford Daily,* they ruled that cops could

[5]*Ibid.,* p. 333.

make a surprise raid, with a warrant, on a newsroom to poke around for evidence of crime committed by others.

In *Saxbe vs. Washington Post,* they ruled that the press has no more right of access to public institutions than any ordinary citizen, like you or me; this opinion was echoed in two other decisions, *Pell vs. Pocunier* in 1974 and *Houchins vs. KQED* in 1978.

In 1976 they made it easier for persons to sue a news source for libel in a ruling in *Time Inc. vs. Firestone.* Two other rulings, in 1979, affirmed this idea.

Do you now see how hard-hitting such examples can be? A string of specific instances may be difficult to find, but such a collection can really bolster your argument. Of course, to be effective, specific instances must be either instantly recognizable by the audience or else self-explanatory, since they are almost a kind of *shorthand.* If they are *not* instantly recognizable by the audience, or not self-explanatory, further detail must be added to explain the instances; that is, the specific instances need to be converted into *illustrations.*

Comparison and Contrast. Comparisons are usually used in a speech to show the similarities of two or more things; contrast is used to demonstrate differences.

Comparisons are generally used to do one of three things: to make meaningful something relatively meaningless; to explain something unknown in terms of something known; or to explain something new and "suspect" in terms of something old and "acceptable."

For instance, take the term *one billion dollars.* Sure, you know that a billion bucks is 1000 times more than a million; you realize that it is twice as much as half a billion and half as much as 2 billion. But is the term *one billion dollars* really meaningful to you? Probably not. You and I are used to handling money a few dollars at a time and can hardly grasp the significance of such a huge sum. (Perhaps that is the reason that a former U.S. Secretary of Defense remarked that it is very difficult these days to spend a billion dollars and get your money's worth.)

To make this term more meaningful, let's compare it to amounts that we can more nearly comprehend. Suppose we had $1 billion to spend, then, and that we were to spend $100 a minute, 60 minutes per hour, 24 hours per day. We wouldn't even stop to eat, sleep, or take a shower. When would we run out of money? After just a little more then nineteen years!

Most people do not know the relative number of "aged" citizens we have in this country; if they *did* know, they might not know the significance of the number. So Louis Haufman began his speech "Older Americans: A National Resource" thus:

> There are 31 million Americans 60 years and older. They constitute the single largest minority in the nation—more of them than there are balcks or Chicanos of all ages.
>
> This minority, since 1960, is growing at twice the rate of our total population.[6]

New ideas and trends are disturbing to most people. If a new idea can be favorably compared with an older, more acceptable idea, it becomes less disturbing. "Federal aid to education" was feared until it was pointed out that we have had it for many years, dating back to the federal land-grant program to provide land for state colleges, the GI bill of World War II, the hot lunch program, and so on.

In the 1960s, America experienced a series of demonstrations on college campuses across the nation. These protests, some of which produced violence and counterviolence, deeply disturbed people, who asked themselves, "How can students so violate their traditional roles as peaceful, thoughtful, inactive vessels to be filled with knowledge?"

Such people must have been unaware of the history of student protest: that a riotous commencement at Columbia University resulted in the students' taking over the church in which it was to be held—and that was in the year 1811! They did not know that the University of North Carolina faculty, in 1851, had to deal with 282 cases of students' delinquent behavior—when the college had only 230 students. They were unaware that half the student body of Princeton had to be suspended in 1807, and that general riots were the standard of the times at the University of Virginia in 1827.

---

[6] Louis Haufman, "Older Americans: A National Resource," *Vital Speeches of the Day,* January 1, 1977, p. 37. Quoted by permission of *Vital Speeches of the Day.*

Student riots and protests may be disturbing to many, but not because they are a new idea!

Contrast is often used to point out the vast difference between a proposed and an actual result. Fred L. Hartley, quoted earlier, blasted big labor and the federal government for waste and inflation with contrast:

> Consider the Humphrey-Hawkins Act which was pushed by labor leaders. It promised 1.4 million jobs, most governmental, to cure unemployment at a cost to taxpayers of $6300 or more per job. . . . Private business during the past two years produced seven million new jobs without a penny cost to the taxpayer.[7]

Testimony.   Testimony has a purpose you must already know and probably have taken advantage of. The idea behind it is that if people won't believe *me*, I will get someone to testify for me whom they *will* believe. For instance, Jenkin Lloyd Jones, a syndicated columnist and professional public speaker, gave a speech in 1973 in which he urged stronger parental discipline as a solution to raising happier children. The speech, "Let's Bring Back Dad: 'A Solid Value System,' " was loaded with testimony from experts on child psychology:

> Robert E. Cavanaugh, writing in a recent issue of *Psychology Today* magazine, says, "The failure of the home, the school, the church to transmit a sound and solid value system further heightens the student identity crisis. Today's student lacks a strong parental figure or a deeply indoctrinated sense of values to give him polarization."
>
> In his book, *Ancient Rome, Its Rise and Fall*, Philip Van Ness Myers says, "First at the bottom, as it were, of Roman society and forming its ultimate unit was the family. The most important feature or element of this family group was the authority of the father. It was in the atmosphere of the family that were nourished in Roman youth the virtues of obedience, deference to authority, and in the exercise of parental authority, the Roman learned how to command as well as how to obey."
>
> Then what happened? Jerome Carcopino in his book, *Daily Life in Ancient Rome*, said, "By the beginning of the second century

[7] Hartley, *op. cit.*, p. 489.

A.D., Roman fathers, having given up the habit of controlling their children, let the children govern them and took pleasure in bleeding themselves white to gratify the expensive whims of their offspring. The result was that they were succeeded by a generation of wastrels." I might point out that after the generation of wastrels came Attila, the Hun.

Robert Paul Smith in his little book, *"Where Did You Go?" "Out" "What Did You Do?" "Nothing,"* had this to say: "I can no longer remember the crisis which involved my son: but in essence, it had reached the point of all arguments where he was saying the hell he would and I was saying the hell he wouldn't. . . . He was two or three. His mother rushed in to say that I must Gesell him a little, or at least Spock him or treat him with a little Ilg, and I went away. . . . I found him later, ready to renew hostilities, but on his face and in his manner was much weariness, much fatigue, and a kind of desperation. I had a moment of pure illumination: I stood there and saw inside his head as clearly as if there had been a pane of glass let in his forehead. What he was saying was, 'Please, please, for Heaven's sake, somebody come and take this decision out of my hands, it's too big for me,' I grabbed him and picked him up and carried him to wherever it was I thought he was supposed to go. He was little then, he hit me and bit me and wet me, he hollered bloody murder and did his level best to kill me. I remember now, it was to his bed he was supposed to go. I got him there, and dumped him in, put the crib side up. He was in his cage, and he had been put there by his keeper, and he went to sleep as happy as ever I saw him. There were rules. Nobody was going to leave him out in the middle of nowhere trying to figure out what he was supposed to do, when he was too young to know what to do."

Another writer says, "Children need and want discipline. Every time they misbehave, they are saying help me; show me how far I can go; don't let me hurt myself."[8]

Everybody has used testimony for "proof" at one time or another, whether in a scholarly and learned term paper in school or in a knock-down, drag-out argument in which is screamed, "Okay, if you don't believe me, you just ask [choose one: my Dad; my teacher; Mr. Jones next door; my Grandma; my boss; my big sister]!"

[8]Jenkin Lloyd Jones, "Let's Bring Back Dad," *Vital Speeches of the Day*, May 15, 1973, pp. 473–476. Quoted by permission of Vital Speeches of the Day.

But there are two other uses to which you can put testimony: to simplify complicated arguments and to spice up your speech.

Suppose you are to give a speech to a general audience on a highly technical and complicated topic, such as the supersonic transport (SST) airplane, or the MIRV missile system, or one of the several SALT disarmament treaties. To prove your point, you might cite the many statistics of cost, danger to the environment, chance of success, and so on and bore your audience to death. You can simplify by citing well-known experts who agree with you. For instance, at present (1980) the man in politics considered the leading expert on arms treaty *monitoring* is Senator John Glenn. If you want to prove that the (currently) proposed SALT II treaty should or should not be ratified, Senator Glenn's testimony on your behalf could save you much time and audience confusion.

Many skilled speakers use quotations to brighten and spice up their speeches. An apt quotation that says just what you wish you had said, and in a manner you would never have thought of, delights the ears of your audience and marks you as a literate and sensitive human being. So, as a speaker, you should have at your elbow when working on your speech one book—or better, several—of such apt quotations. In many books of quotations, these snatches of poetry and condensed wisdom are arranged alphabetically by subject matter and so are easy to find.

Suppose you were to develop a speech in which you advocate "courage to face the future." If you had *my* library, you could find many apt quotes to flesh out that speech. You could open to "Courage" in my *Peter's Quotations,* by Dr. Laurence J. Peter (author of *The Peter Principle*) and find a number of pithy remarks you might use:

> Bravery is being the only one who knows you're afraid.
>
> FRANKLIN P. JONES

> A timid person is frightened before a danger, a coward during the time, and a courageous person afterwards.
>
> JEAN PAUL RICHTER

> Courage is grace under pressure.
>
> ERNEST HEMINGWAY

Dr. Peter provides twinkles of humor, should you wish to use them:

> Coward, n. One who in a perilous emergency thinks with his legs.
> AMBROSE BIERCE

> A coward is a hero with a wife, kids, and a mortgage.
> MARVIN KITMAN

> No call alligator long mouth till you pass him.
> JAMAICAN PROVERB

The Great Quotations, compiled by George Seldes, has no entries under "Courage" but offers under "Brave" a quote from the Roman poet Ovid:

> Through all the air the eagle may roam
> The whole earth is father-land to the brave.

My dog-eared old paperback copy of *Best Quotations for All Occasions,* edited by Lewis C. Henry, offers this gem by Leigh Hunt: "When moral courage feels that it is in the right, there is no personal daring of which it is incapable." And my new *Crown Treasury of Relevant Quotations,* edited by Edward F. Murphy, suggests several:

> What is more mortifying than to feel that you have missed the plum for want of courage to shake the tree?
> LOGAN PEARSALL SMITH

> We learn courageous action by going forward whenever fear urges us back. A little boy was asked how he learned to skate. "Oh, by getting up every time I fell down," he answered.
> DAVID SEABURY

> The highest courage is to dare to appear to be what one is.
> JOHN LANCASTER SPALDING

Books of quotations such as these are simple and easy to use. Take advantage of them, and your speeches will sparkle with glints of wisdom, wit, and charm.

Repetition and Restatement.   You may not consider repetition and restatement supporting material, but the fact is that reiteration to the point of redundant overkill can be extremely useful in planting your ideas in the minds of others. The advertisers certainly use it. They condense their sales pitch into a simple, compelling idea, called a *unique selling proposition* (USP), and assault our senses with it over and over via radio, TV, magazines, newspapers, and so on. Who can forget that "Coke adds life?" Or which cigarette is springtime fresh? Or which beer has "gusto"? Or which is the "king of beers"? We all know which soap is "99 and 44/100ths % pure" ("it floats!"), and which toothpaste produced 27 percent fewer cavities.

Since repetition and restatement do work so well, you should repeat and restate the main points of your speech (the ones you wish your audience to remember) as often as you can without utter monotony. I still remember with clarity a speech a young woman gave in my class twenty years ago. Her point was that children's lives in the United States were overly organized by adults, that kids had no chance to be "just kids" and "mess around" and find out things by themselves. Her speech title, "The Plot Against Childhood," was repeated frequently: "Another aspect of the plot against childhood is . . ." ; "We see further evidence of the plot against childhood in the Little League . . ." ; "Scouting and music lessons are part of the plot against childhood . . ." ; "The plot against childhood also includes Summer Camp . . ." By the time she finished, her entire class perceived parents as little more than scheming saboteurs of their children's lives.

Reiteration works. It *does*. It *certainly* does. Use it!

Definition.   Definition may also seem misplaced in the category of supporting material, but definition is often so used in speech and writing. In discussing "The Future of Capitalism," Milton Friedman, a University of Chicago economist, felt it necessary to clarify any false ideas that his audience might have about the concept of *free enterprise*. Note how much like a supporting argument his definition became:

In talking about freedom it is important at the outset to distinguish two different meanings on the economic level, of the concept of free enterprise, for there is no term which is more misused or misunderstood. The one meaning that is often attached to free enterprise is the meaning that enterprises shall be free to do what they want. That is not the meaning that has historically been attached to free enterprise. What we really mean by free enterprise is the freedom of individuals to set up enterprises. It is the freedom of an individual to engage in an activity so long as he uses only voluntary methods of getting other individuals to cooperate with him. If you want to see how far we have moved from the basic concept of free enterprise, you can consider how free anyone is to set up an enterprise. You are *not* free to establish a bank or to go into the taxicab business unless you can get a certificate of convenience and necessity from the local, state, or federal authorities. You cannot become a lawyer or a physician or a plumber or a mortician (and you can name many other cases) unless you can get a license from the government to engage in that activity. You cannot go into the business of delivering the mail or providing electricity or of providing telephone service unless you get a permit from the government to do so. You cannot raise funds on the capital market and get other people to lend you money unless you go through the S.E.C. and fill out the 400 pages of forms that they require. To take the latest restriction on freedom, you cannot any longer engage in voluntary deals with others or make bets with other people about the future prices of commodities unless you get the approval of the government.[9]

Might your audience harbor any clouded interpretations of your key concepts? Define them. It helps. As Joseph H. Odell wrote in his *Unmailed Letters:*

Few of us pause for definition even in our most serious discussions, and when we do we are amazed, not that there is so much bitter misunderstanding and acrimony in life, but that there is so little.[10]

Description. Description may also not seem like much of a supporting material, but it can be a powerful source of support, es-

[9] Milton Friedman, "The Future of Capitalism," *Vital Speeches of the Day,* March 15, 1977, p. 333. Quoted by permission of *Vital Speeches of the Day.*

[10] As quoted in Edward F. Murphy, ed., *The Crown Treasury of Relevant Quotations* (New York: Crown Publishers, Inc., 1978), p. 206.

pecially after all other kinds of support have failed. Take the thesis of "Drive carefully." How many times have we read the statistics on death and injury on our highways? How many slogans have been run by us (for example, "Arrive alive"; "Drive defensively"; "The life you save may be your own"; "Slow down and live") with almost no effect on our reckless and murderous driving habits. But more than 5 million reprints of an article first published in *Reader's Digest* in 1935 have been handed out to speeders by law enforcement people—because they believe the article will scare drivers into being more careful!

This article was reprinted in a collection in 1940 and reprinted in *Reader's Digest* in 1966. What kind of "support" does it use to scare drivers? Nothing more than a verbal description of what happens to people in automobile crashes. None of that article is quoted here; I choose not to risk upsetting your stomach. But if you would like to read some really scary, gut-stirring description, see J. R. Furnas, "And Sudden Death," *Reader's Digest,* October, 1966.

I will offer a milder descriptive passage, however, this a CLIO award-winning radio commercial. These words were spoken by a man while, in the background, someone's strained, raspy breathing could be heard:

> Every day you inhale fifteen thousand quarts of air — all of it polluted. This polluted air contains: sulphur dioxide, a chemical linked with chronic bronchitis; carbon monoxide which, in sufficient quantities, will kill you; acrolean, a chemical used in tear gas in World War I; benzopirene, which has produced cancer on the skin of mice. Our polluted air also contains unconscionable amounts of dirt and soot. It's come to the point where either you do something about air pollution or air pollution may do something to you.
>
> If you've had your fill of polluted air, send your name to Citizens for Clean Air, Box One Million, Grand Central Station, New York.

Wit and Humor

There have been a number of experimental studies to determine if wit and/or humor act as support in otherwise straightforward speeches to inform or persuade. Many of these studies have been summarized in the last two chapters of my book, *Understanding*

Laughter: The Workings of Wit and Humor (Chicago: The Nelson-Hall Co., 1978). I've summarized the findings of these studies here.

1. The addition of humor to a persuasive speech has not been found to affect persuasion one way or the other, unless the humor used is inappropriate to the subject matter of the speech or otherwise is offensive (such as with sick humor).

2. Use of appropriate humor in optimum amounts in speeches to inform have been very rarely found to enhance the learning of material from the speech; however, the use of humor will probably make the audience "like" the speaker more. Over time this greater "liking" could conceivably result in the speaker's gaining credibility, thus becoming more persuasive with the audience members who know him or her.

3. The addition of sarcastic or satiric wit to an otherwise straightforward persuasive speech has not been found to enhance or detract from a speech's persuasiveness.

4. "Straight" satiric messages, such as those by satirists Art Buchwald, Art Hoppe, or Russell Baker can result in the changing of attitudes (persuasion), but only if the receivers of the messages understand or catch the *serious points* of the satirical messages. How a satire works to achieve persuasion is complicated, and depends upon the ego-involvement in and importance placed upon the satirized topic by the audience member.

5. When speakers mildly "kid" the professions to which they belong, the audience is likely to consider these speakers to be more witty and have a better sense of humor than if they did not so kid their calling.

In short, the evidence suggests that most speakers would do well to leave humor out of their speeches unless they are out to purely entertain an audience or else have had enough experience with the use of humor to know how to use it well. At any rate, humor in most speeches should be served like gravy—sparingly.

Visual Aids. The addition of visual aids to your speech can sometimes help immensely to make your points clearer, more vivid, or more persuasive. A picture may or may not be worth a thousand words (that depends on the quality both of the picture

Figure 1. Mark Harriss Gruner explains the human larynx using an enlarged model of it.

and of the words), but if you can help your audience "see" your points better through visuals, by all means use them.

Figure 1 shows a speaker talking on the structure and workings of the human larynx. Wouldn't the use of that large-scale model of the human voice box make for greater ease of understanding on the part of the audience?

Figure 2 shows another speaker explaining the basics of the Braille system of reading for the blind. The visual aid, carefully made at home on heavy poster board by the speaker, would greatly enhance the appreciation and understanding of this subject so foreign to most of us. Such visual aids, by the way, made up beforehand on poster board or other materials, are usually far superior to those reproduced on the blackboard by the speaker during the speech. The premade visual aid looks better, it saves time, and it allows the speaker to talk to the audience without turning his or her back to them.

Figures 3 through 7 show some other types of visual aids you might use to give your speech a professional look.

Figure 2. Ms. Jeri A. Weaver explaining the Braille system.

Figure 3 shows an exploded drawing, excellent for demonstrating how a mechanical device goes together and operates. Figure 4 shows two circle graphs or pie charts, most useful for the presenting of percentage data. Figure 5 presents the bar graph for showing relative amounts and/or rates. And Figure 6 shows a multiple-line graph, a fine way to show the comparison and contrast between two or more trends (but not *too* many trends, please! Read on). Figure 7 is a good example of the cutaway drawing, highly effective in showing the inside workings of mechanical operations.

Although it is true that the effective use of visual aids can make a veritable blockbuster of a speech, it is also possible for the *attempted* use of visual aids to turn a fair speech into a fiasco. Having been at this racket a number of years, I have been witness to hundreds of student speeches, and I have seen dozens of speeches ruined by the inept use of visuals. Equipment has, frustratingly, refused to work; electrical outlets have been found to be unconnected; posterboard drawings have been so dim or so tiny as to produce eyestrain headaches in the audience; projectors have jammed or their projection bulbs have burned out; electrical cords have not been long enough to reach an outlet;

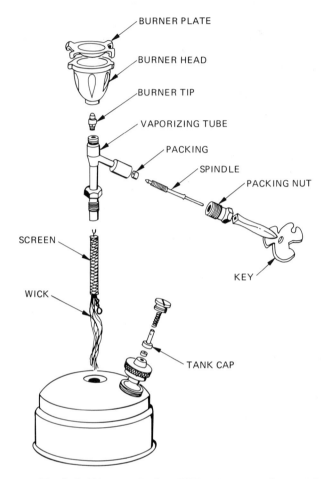

Figure 3. "Exploded Drawing" of an SVEA 123 stove. (*Source:* Reproduced from EMS Catalog, 1971–72, by permission of Eastern Mountain Sports, Inc.)

demonstration materials have slipped from sweat-slickened hands and crashed to the floor; trembling hands have spilled liquids on the speaker and the desk; speakers have suddenly discovered that when the projector is on and the lights out, their speech note cards are unreadable; posters curled up into a tube for transport to the classroom refuse to stand up straight on the chalkboard tray; speakers remove borrowed equipment from its carrying luggage to discover that they don't know how to operate that brand and model. And so on. Can you believe all this? Believe me, I am a personal witness to it all, and more. Therefore I propose the following list of do's and don'ts.

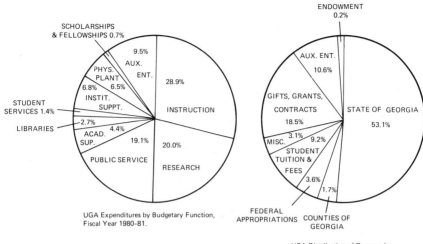

UGA Expenditures by Budgetary Function, Fiscal Year 1980-81.

UGA Distribution of Revenue by Source, Fiscal Year 1980-81

Figure 4. Two examples of circle graphs or "pie charts." (*Source:* Reproduced here by permission of the University of Georgia.)

1. Make posters, drawings, lettering, and so on large and dark enough to be seen. To check, stand back thirty or forty feet from your work. Can *you* see it OK?

2. Keep visuals simple. The audience cannot comprehend anything very complex, and a complex visual will be a distraction.

Figure 5. A Bar Graph. (*Source:* From Walter and Scott, Thinking and Speaking, 3rd Ed. Reprinted by permission of the Macmillan Publishing Company.)

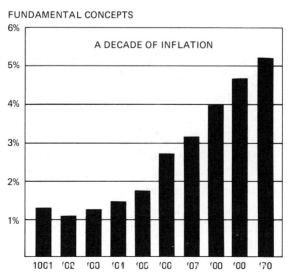

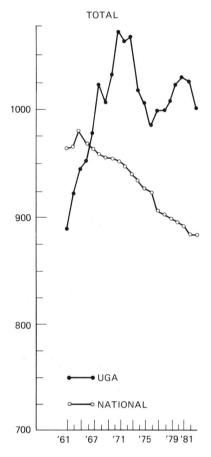

Figure 6. Multiple line graph contrasting average SAT Scores of fall quarter entering freshman to those of all colleges nationwide. (*Source:* Reproduced by permission of the University of Georgia.)

Each person in the audience might be attending to a different part of the complicated chaos, whereas you want them all to attend to the same point at the same time. That's why you are speaking and all of them are listening. Take a look at Figure 8. Now *that's* a visual you should never use in a speech!

3. Remember, the visual aid is for the audience, not you, to look at. You should look at the audience the maximal amount of time, at the visual aid a minimal amount of time.

4. Fight the nervous tendency to play with any visual aid you may have in your hands. This is distracting. Show it, then set it down, or hide it behind the lectern. Don't threaten to skewer

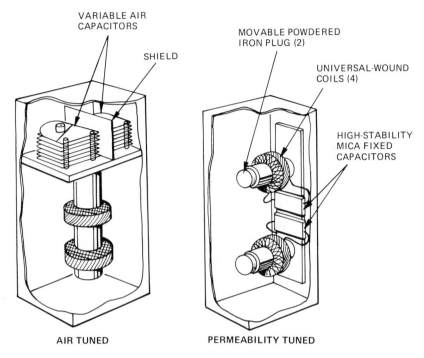

VARIABLE AIR
CAPACITORS

SHIELD

MOVABLE POWDERED
IRON PLUG (2)

UNIVERSAL-WOUND
COILS (4)

HIGH-STABILITY
MICA FIXED
CAPACITORS

AIR TUNED

PERMEABILITY TUNED

Figure 7. Cutaway drawing of two transformer constructions. (*Source:* Reproduced by permission of the American Radio Relay League.)

Figure 8. Example of too much detail for a visual aid to a speech. (*Source:* From Handbook of Geophysics, Rev. Ed. USAF (New York: The Macmillan Publishing Company, 1960), pp. 5–6. Reprinted by permission of the Macmillan Company.)

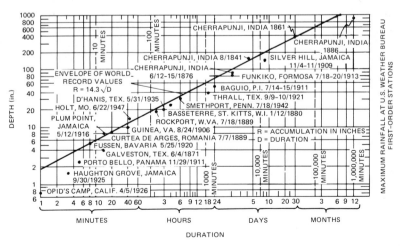

the front row of people with a pointer as you fence with the air, and don't use the pointer for calisthenic exercises as you talk.

5. Use your visuals only when you need to. Keep them out of sight until they are needed, use them, and then get them out of sight again.

6. Rehearse your speech with the visual materials. Make sure you know how to use them. If possible, rehearse with them in the room where you will present the speech.

7. Don't let a projector beat you. A projector has a motor in it that hums; you must learn to speak over that noise. Operate the projector with a long remote-control cord so that you can be up front; then you, not the slides, will dominate the scene. Show slides in only half-darkened rooms, so you can see notes, if necessary (or provide your own shaded light over the lectern). Make sure you have an extra projection bulb in case the one in the machine burns out.

8. Maintain the audience focus of attention on you and the point you are making at any given time. This means, for instance, never pass things around through the audience. Doing this turns a polarized audience attending to you to a buzzing bunch of individuals with individual focuses of attention.

Visual aids should not be dragged in just so that they are there. Some speeches probably cannot be enhanced enough through visual aids to justify the trouble and expense. On the other hand, some concepts might be so difficult to communicate that they absolutely require visual representation.

5

Get Your Skull—and Your Speech—Organized

What do a successful business venture, an effective political election campaign, and a good speech have in common? Good organization. Good organization is particularly necessary in a speech for several reasons.

First, as I noted in Chapter 3, you will remember your speech much better if it is well organized. The finding that well-organized material is easier than unorganized material to learn and remember has been documented in myriad studies. It also follows, then, that the audience will be better able to remember your speech—and they *must* remember it if they are to act on it.

Second, your audience will appreciate the good order in a well-organized speech. If the audience can follow from point to point, seeing that B follows A and that C follows B in logical progression, and if they can deduce the total pattern of your thoughts, they will revel in a kind of aesthetic appreciation. After all, most audience members have sat through many a miserably organized, hard-to-follow speech. Give them one they can easily comprehend, and they will applaud both themselves and you for it.

The third reason for organization in a speech is the most important: it will help ensure the speech's effectiveness.

And what is the "effectiveness" you are trying to accomplish in a speech? You will remember from Chapter 2 that each speech should have one clear-cut purpose, and that to accomplish that single purpose, the speech will usually attempt to get across to the audience just two or three main points or ideas. Proper organization presents those two or three main points in memorable order and should also ensure repetition of those main points often enough to reinforce their retention. This is a very important point. People cannot learn and remember a great deal of material from a speech. If you have a speech that, to be successful, requires the audience to remember seventeen specific facts, that speech will fail. But if all your organization and presentation of details is designed to make them remember the two or three generalizations (your main points) that they must remember (and believe), then your chances for success are great.

In order to facilitate the audience's memory of those two or three generalizations, your speech should be organized in what is called the *partitioning pattern*. Let us look at that pattern, first in the abstract, then applied to several subject matters.

The Introduction

Your speech can begin in any one of a large number of ways. Some of the ways suggested by others are establishing rapport with the audience through reference to the audience, to the occasion, or to yourself; giving a personal greeting; defining some key term in your speech; referring to the title and explaining why you chose it; referring to a previous speaker; presenting a brief history of the topic; telling an anecdote, humorous or otherwise, that illustrates your central theme; narrating a dramatic incident; or quoting from a newspaper, magazine, book, or poem. And there are probably many more ways.

However, there are two objectives that every speech introduction should accomplish. First, you need to provide the audience with your rationale for speaking to them at that time and on that topic. Second, you need to reveal your specific purpose to them. And in doing the latter, you ought to go one more step and reveal to the audience what main points you are going to make in your speech. That is, you need to lay out your organizational pattern so that they can begin to know what you have in mind. In abstract outline form, your introduction, then, should look like this:

> **Rationale:** It's a pleasure to be here. I have chosen to speak to you today on _____ because . . .
>
> **Thesis:** My point in speaking on this topic today is to (inform, convince) you that . . .
>
> **Partitioning:** In order to do this, I will be presenting three major points.
> My first point will be . . .
> My second point will be . . .
> And my last point will be . . .

This kind of introduction provides the audience with the initial motivation to listen carefully, and it reveals your game plan.

Now, of course, there will be some times when you will not want to reveal your exact thesis or major arguments. When? When you are planning to speak on a controversial topic that will arouse initial hostility in your audience. Suppose, for instance, that I began a speech like this:

> I think you will agree with me that tonight I am speaking on a topic that is absolutely vital to every man, woman, and child in this country, because it will touch the pocketbook of each and every one of us.
>
> For tonight, I intend to convince you that the United States should put an additional tax of one dollar on each gallon of gasoline sold. In order to do this, I will present three arguments:
>
> First, there are a number of compelling reasons concerning gasoline supply, demand, and replacing gasoline with substitute fuels.
>
> Second, a one-dollar-a-gallon rise in taxes will solve a number of problems.
>
> Third, the one-dollar-a-gallon tax is the most feasible alternative of those available.

What would happen? All those opposed to the tax would begin mentally arguing with me the minute I finished stating my purpose. The audience attitude? "All right, buster, you just *try* and convince me of that nonsense!" In chapter 9, we will take up the proper way to handle the introduction of such volatile topics. But for now, suffice it to say that the vast majority of your speeches should begin with the rationale for the topic, the thesis statement, and the partitioning of that thesis into its main points before you go on into the body of the speech itself. Emulate A. W. Clausen, President of the Bank of America, speaking at Gonzaga University, November 2, 1978:

> Underlying the weakness of the dollar are profound, long-term problems which need immediate attention.
>
> The need for prompt and effective action adds urgency to the four points underlying my message today:
>
> First, the plight of the dollar has the makings of a real crisis, if in fact it has not already reached those dimensions.
>
> Second, while most Americans may see little direct effect, the "dollar problem" exacts a toll from all of us—a toll that threatens to escalate sharply if the trends of the past few months are permitted to continue.
>
> Third, it's crucial for the United States and for our global neighbors to restore monetary order with dispatch. Currency problems, when neglected, have a way of gathering momentum and reaching "critical mass."

Finally, and most importantly, any effective solution will require us to change some of our ways and attitudes and to exercise much greater self-discipline, individually and as a nation.[1]

The Body

The body of your speech is the meat of your presentation. Here you present your main points and the supporting material for each in the prearranged order you have chosen. And it will help if you can restate each point as often as possible without boring redundancy. For instance:

> You will remember from my introduction that my first point today is to show that our schools are overcrowded and underfinanced. Let's explore that point now. Why do I say our schools are overcrowded? Well, let me quote . . .
>
> So you see, now, that by the most conservative of standards, our schools *are* overcrowded. But are they also underfinanced? I think I can show dramatically just how underfinanced they are. Let me read you the report on . . .

After stating and explaining or proving your first main point, you now need a smooth *transition* to your next point.

Why use transitions? Because audience members appreciate them, and because the audience is led into shifting gears in their heads because the topic is going to change slightly. And we all have become accustomed, through reading, to little signs that the topic is changing. In writing we have chapter headings, subheadings, white space, new paragraph indentations, and so on to let us know that the focus of the subject matter is making a slight turn or jump. Because we do not have these items in speech, we have to provide them, vocally.

A good transition usually summarizes the previous main point and forecasts the next, such as:

> Now that you can see just how overcrowded and underfinanced our schools really are, we can go on to my second point: that we

[1] A. W. Clausen, "The Plight of the Dollar," *Vital Speeches of the Day,* January 1, 1979, p. 162. Reprinted here by permission of *Vital Speeches of the Day.*

can solve both these problems with a modest rise in school taxes. If we were to raise our taxes by only one mil, it would mean that . . .

Your last transition could summarize all previous main points:

> So you see that our schools are crowded and underfinanced, and you probably agree that a one-mil rise in taxes would solve the problem. Now let's go on and explore the question, "Is the tax hike the most advantageous and practical solution?" Well, I think the tax hike *is* the most advantageous and practical of solutions, and here are my reasons: . . .

The Conclusion

The conclusion, at the very least, should again restate or summarize the main points of the speech and restate your purpose or goal.

> I hope that what I have said here tonight has convinced you that our schools are overcrowded and underfinanced; that passage of a one-mil increase in school taxes will solve our problems; and that this increase is the most practical and advantageous of the solutions available.
> Therefore I again ask for your support of the school board in raising our school taxes by one mil.

A conclusion might also include some material for rounding out the speech on a high note. Several techniques are available, such as a prediction of what the future holds; a factual or hypothetical illustration embodying the thesis of your speech; a wise or pithy saying; a vivid quotation; a call to action; a statement of your own personal intent; or a challenge to the audience ("Have you the courage to stand up and be counted?").

In summary, the partitioning pattern I strongly recommend here gives the audience a rationale for listening to the speech; reveals to the audience your purpose and your main points for achieving that purpose; presents each main point in a logical sequence, bolstered with appropriate supporting material; separates the main ideas and reinforces them with sound transitions; and summarizes again the main points and restates the thesis. And when you begin that final summary, the audience will say to itself, "Ah, here's the windup." And once you have restated your thesis after your summary, you will pause; everyone will know that you have ended your speech, and you won't have to clue them in with some tired cliché such as, "Thank you."

This partitioning pattern must have been used by the rural preacher who always sounded so well organized in his sermonizing. One day a parishioner asked, "Reverend, what is the secret of your clear sermons?" The preacher replied, "Well, first I tell 'em what I'm gonna tell 'em; then I tell 'em; and then I tell 'em what I done told 'em." If you do the same, you can't go wrong.

Arranging Main Ideas

There are various ways to arrange main ideas. Some of these are suggested by the topic itself; some are not.

Chronological or time order is suggested by almost any how-to-do-it, or process, speech topic. Main points are simply brought up chronologically in your speech as they occur chronologically in reality.

Purpose: To inform audience of how to secure a passport.

Main Points:
  I. Get a certified birth certificate from your County Clerk.
 II. Find a qualified photographer and get two duplicate photos of yourself.
III. Get a passport application from one of the several places that supply them.
 IV. Send in the completed application, the birth certificate, and the photos, together with a check for $12, to the passport office.

Size order may be suggested by your topic. For instance, in discussing the four poisonous species of snakes in the United States, you might begin with the species most prevalent in the country and end with the one least prevalent, or vice versa.

Spatial or *geographical* order may also be suggested by your topic. For instance, a topic such as "The House I Hope to Build Someday" might be divided into:

I. The general living area
II. The bedroom wing
III. The working space
IV. The grounds

Causal order might be adopted for a number of different speech topics. You can begin with the causes first and give the effects last, or vice versa. For instance, in discussing sickle-cell anemia, you might want to talk first about the symptoms and then explain how they are caused; you could also do these points in reverse.

Problem-solution order is a stock-issues arrangement and has been institutionalized as *the* order for discussing the solution of any problem. The three main points are always the answers to three questions: (1) Is there a problem? (2) Can your plan solve the problem? (3) Is your plan the most practical available? More will be said about this order in Chapter 9 on persuasion, where the motivated sequence is also discussed.

Topical order is the speaker's catchall or miscellaneous order to use when no other order is logically suggested by the subject matter of the speech. The speaker simply divides up the material around several topics that are subordinate to the specific purpose of the speech. For instance, Joan Robertson wanted to explain to her classmates at the University of Georgia the history and significance of the mural on the outside of the Visual Arts Building. She divided her material into three topics:

I. First, I want to tell you something of the life of Jean Charlot and how he came to be artist-in-residence at the University of Georgia from 1941 to 1944.
II. Charlot did the Visual Arts Building mural, entitled "Visual Arts, Drama, Music," as a fresco in three parts.
III. The painting style used by Charlot was influenced by a number of events in his career as an artist.

The Outline

Let us first look at a few rules you should follow in constructing your outline, and then I will present a model outline that follows those rules and that you would do well to emulate in your own efforts.

1. At the top of your outline, you should write down the purpose of your speech or the goal you hope to achieve, in terms of what response you want to get from your audience. (Remember step 2 from Chapter 2.)

> The purpose of this speech is to get the audience to approve my plan.

2. Your outline will be divided, like your speech, into three parts: the introduction, the body, and the conclusion. Begin with the body first, and divide it into the *main ideas* you will need to achieve your purpose or goal (step 3 from Chapter 2).

These main ideas should be stated in complete sentences, usually *simple* sentences with an active verb. These main ideas (like all the ideas stated in the outline) should be worded as you would say them to an audience (not as "notes to yourself"). Your main ideas should be simple, logical divisions of your purpose; they should reflect a simple, consistent, unified thought pattern. In fact, check to see that the set of main ideas, if accepted or understood by your audience, will result in success in achieving your purpose. For example:

I. My plan will benefit workers.
II. My plan will benefit management.
III My plan will benefit consumers. (Note that the Roman numerals denote the main ideas.)

As you divide your main ideas into subordinate ideas, these should usually be indicated by capital letters. These subordinate ideas should also be in complete, simple sentences. Use indentation to show the descending order of generality of ideas and supporting materials, which ought to be included in the outline; this indentation should also show that the subheads at each level develop the heading just above them. And when you divide a section into subheads, make sure there is a true division in the sense that *two* or more parts result from the division (you cannot divide something and have only one thing left; if you have a subhead numbered 1, you must have at least a 2).

I. My plan will benefit workers.
- A. It will benefit workers in unions.
  1. Fact A proves this.
  2. Expert A also agrees with this conclusion.
- B. It will also benefit nonunion workers.
  1. This is proved by Fact B.
  2. Expert B also agrees.
  3. This plan benefited nonunion workers in Canada and England.
     - a. In Canada all wages went up 4 to 5 percent.
     - b. English workers made more money for shorter hours.
- C. Even white-collar workers will benefit.
  1. Expert C testifies to this effect.
  2. A poll of white-collar workers in England indicates satisfaction with my plan as implemented there.

Transition: So you see, my plan will definitely help workers. But in addition, it will be a boon to management.

II. My plan will benefit management. (And so on.)

Note another feature of the good outline: *transitions* are included between the main ideas, in agreement with the advice earlier in this chapter.

After the body of your speech is completely outlined, with main ideas, subordinate ideas, supporting material, and transitions, you may proceed to develop and outline your introduction and conclusion.

Now, as promised, I present a model outline for you to emulate. Others can be found in Chapter 9 and in the Appendix.

The following was an outline for a speech given in my class during the summer quarter of 1979 at the University of Georgia. It is edited and reprinted here with the permission of its author, Mr. Chris Evans.

Purpose: To inform the audience of what to consider when choosing a quality bicycle.

INTRODUCTION

Rationale: "Happiness is pedaling past the gasoline pump line." Approaching is a bicycle boom that could rival that of the early 1970s. Do *you* know what to look for to get the most for your money in a bicycle?

Thesis: You need to understand three basic principles before buying a bicycle:

Partitioning:

Determine your purpose for buying a bike and the environment in which you will ride it.

Choose a proper retailer.

Become familiar with the bike's major components in order to determine overall quality.

BODY

  I. Select a bike according to your own purpose for having one and where you will ride it.
    A. For flat terrain and short distances, a one-, three-, or five-speed would be adequate.
    B. For longer recreational riding or moderate to tough hills, a ten-speed would be the best bet.
    C. You might want a bike you could carry into a bus, a train, or the office.
      1. A folding bike is available for bus and train travel, but it is expensive and not very comfortable.
      2. A bike light in weight can be taken up and down stairs to an office.

Transition: After deciding what kind of bike you want to get, you will need to decide where you will buy it.

 II. Choose a proper retailer.
    A. Purchase where parts and service are available.
    B. A regular bike shop is usually better than a department store.
      1. The bikes are usually of higher quality.
      2. You are more likely to find a bike that fits *you*.
      3. The bikes are assembled more carefully.
      4. These shops have parts and welcome your repair and adjustment business.

Transition: After you decide on the type of bike for you and find some reputable bike shops in your area, the next step is to look for quality.

III. Examine the bike's components to determine overall quality.
  A. The two basic types are touring and racing styles.
    1. Racing style means connections at sharper angles, which shorten the wheel base to about forty inches, giving quicker steering, less shock absorption, and more responsiveness.
    2. In the touring style, the frame angles extend the wheel base to about forty-six inches, promoting great stability for straight-line riding.
  B. The frame is the single most important component, and determines the bike's efficiency and handling.
    1. The best frame is made of fine alloys and is light.
    2. The heavier, less-expensive frames are made of high- and low-carbon steel.
    3. The good frame will be carefully aligned; check that with the wheels off.
    4. The joints of the frame determine quality, too.
      a. Lightweight metals are brazed.
      b. Heavier, cheaper metals are welded.
      c. The very best bikes have overlapping braces at the frame joints.
  C. Consider the wheels, another major component.
    1. Unless riding rough streets, choose lightweight rims.
    2. High-pressure tires lessen pedaling effort but reduce traction and comfort on bumps.
    3. Lower-pressure tires make it harder to pedal but give more traction and comfort.
  D. Other components, such as brakes and seats, usually match the quality of the frame.

CONCLUSION

If you are considering getting in on the biking, take care in selecting the right bike and the right retailer, and check that bike's components.

6

Speak in Words That Folks Understand

MY NASAL LABIAL FOLD
IS IRRITATED BY BACTERIA
LODGED UNDER THE
OUTERMOST EPIDERMIS
OF THAT AREA.

MY NOSE
ITCHES

One evening a woman and her husband were having an angry argument in their penthouse apartment. Exasperated, the man finally blurted out, "My Dear, I ought to *defenestrate* you right here and now." But he did not.

What? How's that? He wanted to de-*what* to his wife?

OK, break out the dictionary. If you can't find it under *d*, look for *fenestrate* or *fenestration* under *f*. Oh, here it is. From the Latin, *fenestra*, meaning "window." The guy had felt like throwing his wife out the window.

You might think I have picked a silly way to begin a chapter on speech language, especially if you remember your Latin and already knew what *defenestration* means. But this example pinpoints a crucial difference between the language of writing and the language of speech.

With a written message, you can take your own sweet time. You can reread it as many times as necessary. You can look up unfamiliar words in the dictionary. You can ponder the thoughts, then reread them, again and again. You can ask others to read the message and tell you what it means to them.

With a spoken message, it is quite different. Speech must be caught instantly. There is no time to ponder an unfamiliar word, no time to turn a sentence's thought over and over in your mind until you unravel the speaker's idea hidden within. Speech is linear; it just keeps on going, and if you stop to think you are left far behind. As another speech teacher many years ago said, written language must be *ultimately* intelligible, but spoken language must be *instantly* intelligible.

Scholars have concluded that there are distinct and real differences between good oral style and good written style, and quantitative studies tend to support those conclusions. The differences are that oral style:

1. Uses shorter sentences.

2. Uses fewer different words or, you might say, a smaller vocabulary. You might write the word *hence* in an essay, but would you say it in conversation or a speech?

3. Uses shorter words, words with fewer syllables. These are usually easier for a general audience to understand.

4. Uses more contractions. Your English teachers forbid you to write *don't* in an essay and insist that you use *do not*. But you rarely speak it this way.

5. Uses more colloquial and "nonstandard" words, and these come and go, changeable as the seasons. As I write this, "the bottom line" is probably overused and on the wane.

6. Uses more self-reference words (*e.g., I, me, myself, and mine*) and more pronouns in general. In typical assigned English essays, you would refer to yourself as "the writer" or "the author of this essay."

7. Uses more qualifying words, such as *however, but, except, and if.*

8. Uses more terms indicating "allness," extreme or superlative words, such as *all, none, always, every, and never.*

9. Uses more repetitions. Words, syllables, sentences are repeated for impact, because the listener cannot go back and "relisten."

10. Uses more terms expressing personal bias, such as *apparently, it seems (appears) to me,* and *in my opinion.*

11. Uses less precise enumeration, especially with large numbers. Where you would write "$9,684,586.45," you would probably *say* "nearly ten million dollars."

12. Uses more guidelines for the listeners' mental processes, including transitions (already discussed in Chapter 5) and enumeration (". . . and my third point is . . ."), internal summaries.

13. Uses an organization that stresses and repeats main points more often than does written style.

As you can see, speech should sound a lot different from written material that is read aloud. So how do you guarantee that you will talk to your audience in an oral style that they can comprehend and appreciate? There are two ways, depending on how you prepare your speech.

First of all, if you will prepare your speeches for *extemporaneous* delivery as explained in Chapter 2, you should have no difficulty with the problems of oral versus written style. If you know your material well and are choosing your words from your head as you stand before your audience, your style will come out as oral, as conversational. That is, it will unless your speech contains written-style phrases, sentences, or paragraphs that you originally wrote into your speech and unconsciously memorized as you rehearsed them over and over.

Second, some experienced (and *most* inexperienced) speakers feel that they simply must have a manuscript before them with every word to be spoken already chosen. Stage fright is the culprit that usually causes this kind of behavior. And if you are not a student in a class whose instructor absolutely requires extemporaneous delivery, you probably *will* have a manuscript. Business people and politicians almost always seem to have to read their speeches.

So if you are to use a manuscript, *how you prepare it is crucial.*

To keep your manuscript speech from sounding like only an essay on its hind legs, *say it first, and then write it.* Gather your materials, outline the speech, and then say it into a tape recorder as if you were talking earnestly to a friend over a cup of coffee or a beer. Talk to that recorder in your normal conversational tone—the way you will eventually be *conversing* with your larger audience. Then copy the speech from the recording. It should be in your own oral style. Now you can polish up the language a bit: remove the *you know*'s, and the *uh*'s, the incomplete sentences, and the unnecessary repetitions. Then you can rehearse from your manuscript over and over so that it is as familiar to you as the feel of your teeth to your tongue.

The Time/Life company has put out a series of films and other materials to train executives to communicate better. One film is called "How to Make a More Effective Speech." In this film a magical genielike pixie, called Master (and played by actor Robert Morse), teaches A. J. Bagshaw to make a speech. Bagshaw (played by actor John Randolph) is a middle-aged executive who has never made a speech and is terrified when his boss assigns A. J. to do so. Master gets him to gather his material, to adapt it to his audience, to organize it into a motivated-sequence order (more about this in Chapter 9), and then to shout it into his recorder. His secretary then types it up, cleaning up the fluffs, and he has his speech to rehearse. His maiden voyage into oratory is a rousing success, and old A. J. is so proud of himself that he almost pops off the buttons of his dinner jacket.

All too often, people have the misguided perception that somehow the language of public speaking must be far different from that of normal conversation. "Oratory" must ring with polysyllabic words, stentorian phrases, and larger-than-life abstractions referring to heroic and mighty events in the History of Humankind.

Fap. Some very few people can get away with such puffery, but there is a very thin line between eloquence and hot air.

You should not try to cross that line, being a beginner. Just use small, common, easy-to-understand words and make yourself understood. A clerk in the U.S. Department of Agriculture might refer to an implement as an "individually operated, hand-held earth excavator." You should call it a spade. (I recently heard a guy on the radio say, "The game was played on a natural surface." Why could he not have said "on grass"?) The Secretary of U.S. Health and Human Services might prefer to say that the HHS is occasionally bothered by "program misuse" and "management inefficiency," but you would probably want to say that the HHS is still plagued by "fraud, abuse, and waste," words now stricken from the HHS's lexicon.

All right, so you agree. You should keep your language simple. But don't get me wrong. Sometimes you need to *work* on your language to make your speech as effective as you want it.

For instance, you may have a speech that is complete except for dissatisfaction with just one or two words. Perhaps you want to replace a particular word that is almost right with one that is exactly right. Well, not *right,* perhaps, but the most correct. Well, not *correct,* either. Let's see. Where's my thesaurus?

Here it is. Let's see now. "Correct," is on page 100. I find, "correct, adj. accurate, strict, perfect, true, unerring. See *Right.*" Hmmm. Let's look up *right.*

Here it is, page 431: "Right . . . becoming, suitable, proper, correct, meet, fitting, seemly, appropriate . . ." That's *it! Appropriate!* Sometimes you will need to dig into a thesaurus and find the most *appropriate* word for your speech.

Also, as a speaker, as a thinker, and maybe as a student, you should never be content with your own vocabulary. The greater your vocabulary, the greater your grasp of ideas; and the more expansive your understanding of ideas, the more clear and incisive and broad should be your vocabulary. Your vocabulary is like a tool chest; the more tools you have and the more varied they are, the more kinds of jobs you can do.

To actuate you to vary and expand your vocabulary tool chest, I print here a speech by one of my students. It was presented in my class on March 7, 1980, by Mr. Kingsley Corbin, who gave me his permission to edit and reproduce it in this book. Read it for the language and ideas, and then come back later and look at it again as a good model speech using the motivated sequence when you are studying Chapter 9. (Note: Labels in italics in the left margin specify the steps and substeps in the motivated sequence.) *persuasive*

Swell Your Vocabulary, Stretch Your Mind

ATTENTION STEP

The father of a good friend of mine is a real optimist. Last quarter, when my friend's grades from college were mailed, my friend's dad looked at the three F's and one D and said to his wife, "Well, that's a relief—at least we know he isn't cheating in school or taking any of those mind-expanding drugs!"

General Purpose

Well, today I want to talk to *you* about expanding *your* minds—but not through drugs, through vocabulary.

NEED STEP
Statistics
Personal Illustration

If you're an average adult, your vocabulary is barely one-and-one-half times that of a child of ten. Get that? The average adult's vocabulary is only about one-and-one-half that of a ten-year old! And this means something else: it means that your vocabulary is now increasing at a present rate of only one hundredth of the rate while you were in the lower grades of elementary school. Now, if these accusations sound insulting, I am sorry—I'm especially sorry, since they refer to me, too! I used to think I had a good vocabulary until I took a little test a few weeks ago; I found out that my vocabulary is little better than average.

I'm only trying to get you to face the facts about vocabulary development that educational testing studies have turned up in recent years. I'm talking about hard-working scientists interested in the power of words, too, not research by some theoretical English profs over in Parke Hall.

Now, as we're college students, our vocabularies are probably stronger than the average adult's, but I'm sure you would agree that a better vocabulary would sure come in handy for each of us.

Ramification
Illustration
Added Examples

For instance, it's been proved that vocabulary is one indication of intelligence. Learning power definitely improves as vocabulary increases. In one study, two high school classes were selected for an experiment. One class took normal courses, and the other took them plus a rigorous vocabulary training course. At the end of the experiment, the grades in the class with the vocabulary training were much higher. And not only in English; their grades were better in all other courses, including sciences and math. Also, Professor Louis M. Turman of Stanford University has found that vocabulary testing is as good a measurement of intelligence as the standard, accepted Stanford-Binet IQ tests.

And limited vocabulary doesn't just affect schoolwork. It may affect career success later in life. Dr. Johnson O'Connor of the Human Engineering Laboratory of Boston and the Stephens Institute of Technology in New Jersey gave a vocabulary test to a hundred young men studying to be industrial executives. Five years later, without exception, every one of those who passed in the upper 10 percent—that is, those in the upper 10 percent in vocabulary—had attained executive positions. On the other hand, not a single one of those scoring in the lower 35 percent of the vocabulary test had become execs.

"Pointing"

So there you have it. If you folks have good vocabularies, you will probably do well here in school and later on when you go into your careers. And if you don't have good vocabularies, you may have to settle for a C average and a mediocre job after school. But if you have a weak vocabulary, are you doomed to mediocre grades and a mediocre job? Not really. You can do something about it. *Now.*

SATISFACTION STEP
Statement of Action to
Take
Explanation of Action

You *can* improve your vocabulary and do it a whole lot faster and easier than you might ever have imagined. You can do it by using any number of useful books on vocabulary training. I just happen to have a couple right here: [holding up] *Thirty Days to a More Powerful Vocabulary* and *Word Power Made Easy.* Either or both of these books can be purchased in our campus bookstore or at any of the bookstores downtown for $2.25 each.

These books have short quizzes to give you an idea of how good or bad your own vocabulary is. I found out, to my chagrin, that mine was way below what I had thought it was. Then I read about how my vocabulary was going to affect my grades and probably my career after school, and I really began to read them in earnest.

How It Solves Problem

These books don't define words the way a dictionary does. This is not like reading a dictionary. These book tell stories about words. They show how words are related to objects and to other words, and they make a fun game in

Examples

doing so. The more I read, the more I wanted to read.

About a month ago I read in *Thirty Days* the story of the word *obsequious*, which means "excessively polite behavior designed to get something out of you," sort of. Shortly after, I took my girl friend to dinner, and about halfway through, I was able to note that our waiter was quite *obsequious* in his desire to get a big tip out of me. I didn't have to use the expression "excessively polite" or "unnaturally and overly fawning" or some such. That new word is now a permanent part of my growing vocabulary.

It Works

These books are based on two simple principles: (1) words are verbal symbols of ideas; and (2) the more ideas you are familiar with, the more words you will know. These aren't just old, useless books that only a few people use. *Thirty Days to a More Powerful Vocabulary* was first copyrighted in 1942 and is now in its forty-fourth edition. Over four million copies have been sold, so you can bet that *someone* has found it pretty useful!

Overcoming Objections

These books are cheap paperbacks, so you know they're not going to break your wallet. Either one costs less than three packs of cigarettes.

Also, they don't take a lot of time. You can carry them around in your pocket or purse and read them in spare moments. I read half of one chapter on the campus bus from Russell Hall to North Campus, and the other half on the ride back.

Plus, they're not hard to read. Either of these books is a lot easier to read than the textbook for this class [by Gruner *et al.!*] and a whole lot more fun. Since reading these myself, I have seen words in my regular classroom readings that I know, but that I would have just skipped across a couple months ago. Just last night I was reading my psych book and came across the word *misogyny*. Two months ago I would have just let my mind flicker at that word and go on; but now I know from a little word game in one of these good books that *misogyny* means "hatred of women." And man, that's not me. I *love* women!

VISUALIZATION STEP

Just imagine yourself making A's and B's in all your classes beginning next quarter because you understand more clearly what you read in your textbook and hear in your lectures. Or imagine being the manager of a business or a top executive in a company simply because you have a clearer understanding of the instructions and ideas given you by a higher officer. Being on the dean's list and catching the brass ring in the business world sure beat mediocre grades and treadmilling it in the old rat race. The choice is yours.

ACTION STEP

So, what'll it be? Mediocrity, or excellence? Strive to improve your word power. Any good vocabulary book like these will do the job for you—and provide you with some fun at the same time. You might think, "Well, I can do that anytime." But don't put it off. Begin right away. Get down to the bookstore and pick up *Thirty Days to a More Powerful Vocabulary* for only $2.25. Then, when the spring quarter starts, you'll be almost finished with it and ready to take the University of Georgia by storm. *Do* it!

Vividness. If a memorial to John F. Kennedy were to be erected in Washington and adorned with his best-remembered words, what lines would be chiseled into that marble? Probably, "Ask not what your country can do for you—ask what you can do for your country." JFK spoke this figure of speech, called *antithesis*, in his presidential inaugural address.

What are the best-remembered words of the century's master orator, Sir Winston Churchill? There are many, but I vote for "We shall fight on the beaches, we shall fight on the landing grounds, we shall fight . . ." This is the rhetorical tactic of repetition and parallel structure. Martin Luther King, Jr., used the same tactic in Washington, D.C., to bore into the racist conscience of America: "I have a dream . . ."

We mostly remember speakers for a few vivid, ringing words, some catchy figure of speech, or an unusual juxtapositioning of words. Franklin D. Roosevelt's "a date that will live in infamy" and "the only thing we have to fear, is fear itself" are examples. We remember William Jennings Bryan for his "cross of gold" analogy and Teddy Roosevelt for his admonitions to pursue "the strenuous life" and to "speak softly and carry a big stick."

Some of the more memorable speeches of my students stick in my mind because of some figure of speech, a freshly coined word, or some play on words. I remember one young man condemning Communist governments everywhere for their stifling of freedom of communication of all kinds. He called Communism "the cause that represses." A young man extolling the virtues of his home state of Vermont brightened his speech with, "If autumn in Vermont were a woman, every man would leave his wife." A young woman at the University of Nebraska whose family had recently moved to the urbanized east coast complained bitterly in her speech about the loss of rural and small-town advantages. "The national flower of this country," she said, "should be the concrete cloverleaf."

You, too, can spice up your speech and make it memorable with just one or two such jewels. Like me, you may find it difficult to make up your own verbal flashes, but you ought to be able to *find* such bright highlights for your speech. I have already mentioned reference books of quotations (Chapter 4) that contain many. But you can also collect them from your own reading, or even from such sources as the *Reader's Digest's* "Toward More Picturesque Speech" page.

Just as one can make up for a deficient vocabulary by consulting a thesaurus, one can make a speech come to life with borrowed figures of speech.

Figures of Speech. Let's consider a few types of figures of speech and see how they can enliven your talks. The list presented here is not complete, but it typifies the kinds of figures of speech most often used in speeches.

1. *Allegory* is not often used in speeches, but it is a technique that can effectively pinpoint human foibles and shortcomings. An allegory is a story with a figurative meaning. For instance, suppose a speaker is talking about someone who became famous just because he happened to have the great good fortune to be in the right place at the right time. The speaker might say something like:

> Mr. _____ always reminds me of the tale of two grubworms. These two grubworms lived in the ground, and one day the soil in which they lived was picked up on a shovel and carried several yards. On the way, one grubworm fell off into a dark, dank crack in the sidewalk, where he nearly wasted away from lack of food and fresh air. The second grubworm fell off a yard further away and right into a pile of manure, where he flourished and grew fat.
>
> One day, the starving grubworm managed to crawl out of the dark, dank crack in the sidewalk and drag himself over to the manure heap, where he saw his friend. "Oh Brother Grubworm," the frail creature cried, "I have fallen upon hard times. But you have grown prosperous, fat, and sleek. How did you manage to reach this prosperous state?"
>
> The fat grubworm replied, "Oh, just brains and ambition, Brother Grubworm. Just brains and ambition!"

2. *Alliteration* is the repetition of the same sound in two or more consecutive words. The old political epithet of "Rum, Romanism, and Rebellion" is a good example. It sometimes pays to use alliterative words in the title of your speech. I still remember vividly a student speech from several years ago on the "Red menace." It was entitled, "The Communist Criminal Conspiracy." Song titles are often alliterative: "Tea for Two," "It Takes Two To Tango," "Bewitched, Bothered, and Bewildered" come to mind.

3. *Analogy* is the relating of one thing or attribute to another; often the two things being related are actually incomparable in a literal sense but are alike figuratively. To say that balancing the federal budget now would be like locking the barn door after the horse has run off is to compare two really incomparable points, but the analogy makes the financial point clearer. I once made a more literal analogy when I compared a young man's delivery of a speech to that of a clerk: "Your delivery was about as enthusiastic as that of a K-Mart cashier's 'Will that be cash or charge?'" Abraham Lincoln urged voters, "Don't change horses in the middle of the stream," meaning don't change Presidents in the middle of a war.

4. *Antithesis* has already been mentioned. This is a contrast of ideas, sometimes by a simple switching around of words. A good antithetical statement can ring in the heads of your audience for a long time. I once heard a speaker say, "What we need is Congressmen who can not only count votes, but whose votes will count." Our ambivalent feelings toward the ubiquitous telephone were aptly summarized by sociologist Robert Lynd. He described the phone as "the greatest convenience among nuisances, and the greatest nuisance among conveniences."

5. *Epigrams* are brief, witty statements with an unexpected turn. Many of these can be found in collections of quotations. For a speech to a group of authors I gleaned the following:

No author is a man of genius to his publisher.

HEINRICH HEINE.

Almost anyone can be an author; the business is to collect money and fame from this state of being.

A. A. MILNE.

What an author likes to write most is his signature on the back of a check.

BRENDAN BEHAN.

6. *Epithets* are names or adjectives attached to a person or thing that supposedly express some quality or trait of that person or thing. Ring Lardner's famous short story "Alibi Ike" was about a ball player who made excuses constantly, even for things he did well. After James Brown's record popularized the song "Bad, Bad Leroy

Brown," who was "meaner than a junkyard dog," the football fans at the University of Georgia promptly dubbed the defensive unit of their Georgia Bulldogs "The Junkyard Dogs."

Epithets sometimes carry so much magic that they endure like granite even though they are false. Chicago, for instance, is called "The Windy City" but actually ranks only about thirty-fifth among American cities in average wind velocity. The city was saddled with the epithet in the nineteenth century because of a Chicago Congressman who was overly talkative, or windy. General Douglas MacArthur was one of the bravest military officers ever, constantly exposing himself to enemy fire in order to see what was going on at the cutting edge of battle. But he is remembered by many of his former troops as one who always placed the highest premium on his own safety because of the epithet hung on him: "Dugout Doug."

7. *Hyperbole* is something we all use a million times a day. It is excessive exaggeration, overshooting, stretching the truth so much that no one will miss the intended excess. "I Cried a River" is a hyperbolic song title. Billy Sunday, the prohibitionist evangelist, yearned to make America so "dry" (of liquor) that "You'll have to prime a man before he can spit!" Many jokes depend on hyperbole for their impact. An old-timer in the drought-stricken Southwest United States complained, "If it would only rain just oncet! Not for me, mind you—I don't care about me, but it's for my grandchildren. I've *seen* rain!" The "tall tales" we have often enjoyed also depend on hyperbole, as do so many of our "insult" one-liners: "He's so cheap he'd skin a flea for its hide and tallow"; "She's so ugly that when she enters a room, the mice jump up on the chairs"; "He has a face you don't want to remember and can't forget."

8. *Metaphor* is giving a thing the name of something else that it is like. We refer to a problem spot in the highway that creates congestion as a *bottleneck*. And as Harry Reasoner has said on TV, a traffic reporter once mistakenly referred to a spot as "the biggest bottleneck" he had ever seen. Unconscious of the metaphor, the reporter had reversed the meaning. He really meant the smallest bottleneck, but his listeners understood.

We all use metaphors as unconsciously. We might refer to an exciting book as "real dynamite." Our home is our "castle."

An attractive girl is a "vision" or a "doll." A fiancé is "number one on the (top 40) charts."

One danger of using metaphors in speaking is that many are old, overused, and thus trite. If you can invent your own apt, telling metaphors, so much the better. The creative eye that can see a heretofore hidden relationship and uncover it for an audience is much appreciated. Native inventiveness is required to see that original relationship and to transform it into language. For instance, here's what Shana Alexander saw at the bail hearing that preceded the trial of kidnapee-turned-urban-guerrilla Patty Hearst:

> I saw her first from the back, facing the judge, one tiny hand hooked in her jeans. Standing before the high bench, she looked slouching and tough, a transvestite Dead End Kid in lilac tee shirt and dyed red hair. The only way I could see her at all in the packed courtroom was to rise on tiptoe for a quick peek. Other spectators did the same, and throughout these tense proceedings the surface of our dense human throng rose and fell like a pot of bubbling oatmeal.

When sex therapists Drs. Masters and Johnson got chatty on a TV talk show, Alexander saw them as "a happily married couple, just plain Bill and Gini, the Ma and Pa Kettle of Gynecology." Robert Mardian, of the Watergate scandal, she perceived as "a man of Teflon, cold and perfectly smooth."

An infrequent but occasional danger of metaphor is that a speaker might overdo things. Several years ago then-Congressman Gerald Ford got carried away with a "ship" metaphor in attacking the Democratic President. What follows is a transcription of that metaphorical attack and the comments of Harry Reasoner on the 1968 CBS-TV presentation "The Strange Case of the English Language": This transcription is reprinted by permission of the Columbia Broadcasting Company.

> REASONER: Congressman Gerald Ford · got carried away with a "ship" metaphor one night.
>
> FORD: The President's only explanation was, "When a great ship cuts through sea, the waters are always stirred and troubled." Apparently the President has been standing on the stern [pause

for laughter, then applause] looking backward at the wake, wondering which of his officers to dump overboard next. [More
laughter, then applause.]

REASONER: So far, so good. The metaphor worked, so he went on
with it.

FORD: The Ship of State is wallowing in a storm-tossed sea, drift-
ing toward the rocks of domestic disaster . . .

REASONER: . . . and *on* with it . . .

FORD: . . . tossed by the waves of a worldwide fiscal crisis. The
captain should return to the bridge . . .

REASONER: . . . and *on* with it . . .

FORD: We need a captain who will seize the helm, call up full
power, break out new charts, hold our course steadfast and bring
us through the storm.

REASONER: Three minutes later he was *still* going on with it.

FORD: It's time for all hands to man their action stations. Let's not
give up the ship . . .

REASONER: . . . people were beginning to feel seasick . . .

FORD: . . . America has weathered many a terrible storm, rescued
many a weaker vessel, and we'll do it again.

9. *Metonymy* is the use of one word to suggest something else.
It is a kind of metaphor, naming not the object but something related
to it. We refer to "five o'clock shadow" for the trace of whiskers
toward the end of the day. (My son Mark refers to "Tuesday shadow"
after shaving on Saturday!) To say "she cuts a mean rug" meant, in
my day, at least, "she dances well." We will all be well off "when our
ship comes in." Included in metonymy, presumably, would be eu-
phemisms. To "pass away" is less jarring than "to die." We do not
"rest" in "rest rooms," but we do not wish to refer to what we
actually do. But we feel better, as if we *had* rested.
we *had* rested.

10. *Oxymorons* are combinations of contradictory words. We
might say that a particular act was a "cruel kindness" (or vice
versa); we note that the world contains many "educated fools";
almost everyone knows a "poor little rich girl" or has been very
"busy doing nothing."

11. *Understatement* is the opposite of hyperbole, a trick to draw attention to something. A young boy returns home with a black eye, two teeth missing, bruises, and his clothes in tatters. He tells his parents, "I had a little playground misunderstanding with a guy today."

12. *Rhetorical questions* are those that require no answer or that contain their own answers. They are of great use to the speaker for purposes of maintaining audience attention. We have become conditioned to come alive, to wake up when asked a question. In school, as students, we have all been subjected to the teacher's questioning tactic of firing into the crowd. You know what I mean. The teacher asks, "And who knows the year of the Norman invasion of England?" The teacher then thoughtfully scans the faces of the students, trying to find the guilty face of one who does not know the answer. And all the time those ignorant of the date requested by the teacher are furiously rummaging through their memories for that elusive year. After so many years of such conditioning, we, like Pavlov's dogs, respond automatically. But instead of salivating, we throw mind and attention span into high gear when confronted with a sentence beginning with an interrogatory word and ending in the rising inflection of the question. The speaker asks, "Now, just why do you think it was that our Congress passed this bill?" The audience responds, "Yes, just why *did* they?" And audience alertness increases accordingly. This mental stimulation occurs even when the rhetorical question is merely the form into which a factual statement is made, such as: "*Did you know* that lettuce is what we call a 'metabolic' food? That it requires more energy to eat than it provides in calories?"

Do you now see how rhetorical questions and other figures of speech can enliven your speeches?

Summary

Use vivid language and figures of speech to make your speeches memorable, but as you would use spice in cooking: sparingly. Otherwise keep your language simple and conversational. Remember, good speaking is merely enlarged conversation.

I was pleased to read in a book on psychotherapy (*Decision Therapy*) recently of the author's discovery along these lines. He had been an able public speaker from the age of four. He had won medals for speaking in grammar and high school. He had been an intercollegiate debater in college. And yet, after one of his speeches on psychology, he was driving home with a friend, when the friend

> asked me some questions about my lecture, and when I got through answering them, he said, "Why don't you talk as simply as this when you talk to an audience?"
>
> I said, "It has to be larger than life; you have to get their attention." But then I thought about it and made a decision to try it; I would speak to any audience the way I speak to anybody else in ordinary conversation.

The young man who changed his speaking style is Dr. Harold Greenwald, world-famous speaker, psychotherapist, and best-selling author. He found the "plain talk" formula so successful that he decided he would also speak to his clients in plain language. He feels that such plain talk is much better, not only for communication in therapy sessions, but in establishing empathy with the client; he also feels it establishes his *authenticity* with the client far better than donning the traditional mantle of superiority over the patient.

Chat with your audiences; converse with them. They'll *love* it.

7

Stand Up, Speak Up: Keep Your Audience Awake—Perhaps Even Interested

Every speech textbook is obliged to have a chapter on delivery, that is, how a speaker should and should not look and sound before an audience. If all the advice already offered in this book is followed, you will have little need for a chapter on delivery. If you prepare your speeches diligently, with the proper attitude, and decide to approach your audiences with a strong and sincere desire to communicate information and ideas of real worth to them, you should have little need for advice on how to look and sound as you face your audience.

Did you ever see a person interviewed on television at the scene of a strike or a protest meeting? Did you notice that that person had no trouble at all communicating dissatisfaction, anger, even rage to the TV audience? That person believed so strongly in the spoken message that it probably came across as darned-near *eloquent*.

I once watched the live television coverage of a public hearing on a proposed new "urban renewal" project in downtown Watertown, New York. One speaker against the proposal was a small, old, balding little man with a foreign accent. He explained in broken English how, if his building were torn down, his little cigar and candy business would be gone forever, because the building planned to replace it would be too expensive for him to rent space in. He stood in a worn old overcoat, his cap in his hand. Yet his appeal was aurally and visually compelling. Twenty years later I still remember that little guy and his eloquent plea. To paraphrase the editors of *Fortune* magazine, "If you have something to say, and mean it, and feel it as you say it, your audience will understand."

Still, beginners want to know how to look and sound in front of an audience. So I will try to tell them. But remember, it is awfully difficult for me to sit here at a typewriter and give advice on how to deliver a speech to a reader like you, sitting out there looking at black marks on white pages. If I were standing in front of you, live and in color, I could demonstrate what to do and not do; I could get you on your feet and have you perform, then tell you what was good or bad about what you did. I could coach you the way a basketball mentor coaches his players. But I am stuck now with only the printed page as my medium. However, even with this handicap, I think I can get across some ideas, concepts, and tips that you can use to improve your physical speech delivery—at least, in your early speeches, if you are a beginner.

Vocal Delivery

You will remember from previous chapters that you ought to think of public speaking as enlarged conversation. If you are to converse with your audience, then, let's use some common sense in determining how you should sound by comparing the use of the voice in public speaking and the use of the voice in conversing.

Rate.   How fast do you converse? Probably around 120 to 150 words per minute, which is a pretty ideal rate. What if you talk a great deal faster than that? How do others perceive you if you race along at 200 words a minute or faster? That's right: you're seen as being "nervous" or "high-strung," perhaps as being one who feels there is no substance in the language you use, so you are forced to pour it forth in a torrent to prevent criticism of your lack of substance. The very term *fast talker* is considered a negative epithet. And remember, in a public speaking situation your stage fright is apt to make you talk even faster than normal. So watch your speed.

How about if you talk too slowly? What is the common stereotype of the person who drawls and drags words out at a snail's pace? Dim-witted. Stupid. Uneducated. Indecisive. Backward. You get the picture. So keep your pace up, and you will keep your audience's interest—and respect—again, if you don't go *too* fast.

Volume.   What kind of adjectives flash through our minds as we encounter one who talks too loud? How about *overbearing? Lordly? Domineering? Dictatorial? Insolent? Haughty? Arrogant?* Good enough for starters. How about the speaker who makes us strain to hear? The one with the soft voice with barely the strength to vibrate our eardrums? How do we describe such a speaker? *Timid? Diffident? Timorous? Faint-hearted? Fearful, weak, pliant, shy, bashful, demure?* We don't want these labels, either, do we?

The proper action, of course, is to speak loudly enough to be heard easily, but not so loudly that you appear to be overbearing. Remember, in public speaking you will need to converse a little more loudly and with more force than you would to one person on the other side of a card table. As one speaker said, a speech should be directed to a slightly deaf little old lady in the sixteenth row. It just plain takes more energy to speak to twenty or a hundred people than it does to one or two. After you have done a little speaking, this fact will become self-evident. But don't shout at your audience, unless you do it once in a while to emphasize a key point. Do *you* enjoy being yelled at?

Quality. I am going to assume that the quality of your voice falls somewhere in the "normal" range. It is not overly high or low; not too gruff or squeaky; that you can pronounce and enunciate the forty-six or so English phonemes (the individual sounds that make up our language). If your voice is not within the normal range, you probably know it already, and nothing I can write here is going to change it. If you have a serious voice or diction problem (which takes your voice out of the range of normality), you need the help of a professional speech correctionist.

At the same time, I am going to assume that you do not have the charming, compelling voice of a Dan Rather or a Lauren Bacall. In other words, you have a normal speaking voice that is identifiably yours but that, if used to make a speech on a topic you are highly interested in, would not draw so much attention to itself as to interfere with your communicating your message.

And an earnest, communicative attitude on the part of the speaker can go a very long way toward concealing any minor defects of voice or articulation that the speaker might actually have. A young man in my class, a better-than-average speaker, recently asked if he could come to my office and hear his speech, which I had just taped. During the playback, he complained, "I didn't know I had that lisp!" I replied, "Neither did I, until you just called my attention to it." And then I reminded him that the century's greatest orator, Winston Churchill, had a very pronounced lateral lisp, which almost no one noticed because of what Churchill said and how forcefully he said it. Abraham Lincoln, a pretty fair country orator, is supposed to have had a high, reedy voice. It did not stop him!

Pitch. Pitch is how high or low your voice is. An overly high voice in a man is perceived often as "feminine," and a deep, low voice in a woman is often considered "masculine." Again, I assume that your pitch is roughly suitable to your sex and size; if not, there is little I can do about it. You can, through practice, raise or lower your own optimal pitch three or four notes, but to do much else, you need professional help. Otherwise, we all pretty much have to live with the voice pitch dictated by the length and thickness of our vocal folds.

Vocal Variety. Vocal variety is the key to using the voice to hold an audience without a rope. Your rate should vary from quite fast, in running over a minor trivial point in your speech, to slowing down to a pronounced crawl on an important point you need to emphasize, as in "And now—the one—most important—single, solitary thing—that you must remember—is—do not—under any circumstances—touch that—red— switch."

The experienced speaker also uses the pregnant pause for emphasis and variety. A sure sign of the inexperienced speaker is the even, and evenly fast, completely pauseless rate of speech; it is ever so clear that the poor soul's main concern is to finish that speech as soon as possible and sit down and become an audience member again!

The experienced speaker will also vary the speech volume according to the importance or the materials. Some points will need to be literally shouted at the audience; other points can draw more attention to themselves if almost whispered to the audience, especially if accompanied by a conspiratorial facial expression and a slight, intimate lean of the body toward the audience.

A good speaker also diversifies vocal quality. "The enemy that is boring from within" might be rasped out at the audience with a near growl of harshness. But the good speaker might also use the most "theatrical" of pear-shaped tones in hyperbole when talking about, "And now—I present the one—the only—the fabulous single idea of the century . . ."

I think very little needs to be said about variety of pitch. If you *have* variety of pitch (intonation), it is called *melody.* If you don't, it is called *monotone.* And that is monotonous. You need the rising and falling inflection; your voice might fairly *screech* on "Can you imagine that?" Whereas your pitch may drop to its lowest point on a note of solemnity: "And thus his wasted life came to an end after barely twenty-four years."

In short, your voice needs to vary to fit the varying emotional and intellectual levels of your speech's content as you say it. The voice and the content must fit, must be consonant with one another—they must both say the same thing. Variety is the spice of life, they say. Vocal variety in your speech is No-Doz to the audience.

Visual Delivery

Those points already made about vocal delivery can be repeated here about visual delivery, that is, how you *look* as you speak. First, like your vocal delivery, your visual delivery should be varied. You need not stand the same way, in the same place, using the same gestures and facial expression. A lively, varied visual delivery, combined with variety of vocal delivery, will keep your audience attentive.

Visual delivery, like vocal delivery, needs to be consonant with your words and ideas. A smirking grin accompanying a serious point in your speech makes it hard for the audience to take you seriously. Staring out the window or at the back wall while urging immediate action from the audience, which your eyes are avoiding, will not get many rears into gear.

Public-speaking visual delivery, like public-speaking vocal delivery, should resemble the best of conversational delivery. When conversing with someone on a serious topic, we usually expect the bodily posture of our partner to indicate alertness, interest, and yet comfortableness. We want our conversational partner to look at us, to communicate meaning and emotion to us by gestures, facial expressions, changes in posture, and so on.

Before briefly discussing each of the important aspects of visual delivery, let us consider the concept of empathy.

Empathy is the reacting of your own personality to another person you are interacting with in some way so that you feel the way that other person does. When you are sitting in the stands at the football game, and the fullback goes crashing into the line and collides head-to-head with an opposing tackle with a great THWOCK, your cringe of mock pain in sympathy with the full-back is empathy. When you experience the pain and tension of a good friend or your sibling, or child's nervousness in his or her first piano recital, that is empathy, too.

Whenever you get up to speak, your audience is going to empathize with you: if you are calm, poised, and relaxed, they will be poised, calm, and relaxed; if you are bright, alert, and active, they will be bright, alert, and active. If you are sloppy in speech content or delivery, they will be sloppy of mind and attention. As I said above, you cannot help but communicate when you stand before an audience; and you cannot help but cause an audience to think and feel as you think and feel. As speaker and writer Jenkin Lloyd Jones has said, much negative communication between speaker and audience is caused by "stagefright, a virulent affliction among the young. The frightened speaker transmits his agony to the audience. Sympathetic audiences cannot concentrate on what is being said and the whole affair is a fiasco."[1]

Let's look at some aspects of visual delivery that result in positive empathy.

Eye contact with the audience is absolutely essential. You must look into the eyes of each person in your audience, over and over again. Keep your eyes roving around the room, leaving out no one. People want to feel they are being talked to. The only way to ensure that feeling in a live public-speaking audience is to look into their eyes as you speak. It is of paramount importance, then, that you know your speech backward and forward, so that you must spend only a minimal amount of time glancing down at your notes. If you must stick your nose into a manuscript constantly, you communicate to the audience, "I don't know this stuff very well, do I? Why should *you* be very interested if *I* am not."

Your *posture* should be such that the very best possible label that could be applied to it is alert. You should absolutely radiate alertness. This means you will not have one or more hands

---

[1] Jenkin Lloyd Jones, "Short Course in Public Speaking," *Greenville* (SC) *News*, November 28, 1970. Reprinted here by permission of Mr. Jones.

tucked into pockets or belts; you will not hold your hands behind your back or clasp them together in front of you; you will not wring your hands above the lectern; you will not lean on or drape yourself around the lectern; you will not even stand tentatively on one foot, perhaps with the other crossing it or balancing on toe tip behind you, while keeping your balance with both hands on the lectern.

Instead, you should stand tall and erect, on both feet, with the weight of your body more on the balls of your feet than on your heels and thus with a slight lean forward toward the audience. Your feet should be slightly apart, with one slightly forward of the other, for good front-to-back and lateral balance. As a professor of mine once said, "Stand so that if you should faint or die, you would fall toward the audience."

If you have no lectern, hold your notes in front of you with one hand and let the other hang naturally at your side; it will be there ready for any gesture you may feel the urge to make later (it won't be hidden away in a pocket, for instance). If you have a lectern, place your notes on top of it, and with your hands, lightly grip its top at each side. Then, if you should get the urge to gesture, your hands will be "handy."

Your *facial expression,* as mentioned above, should be consonant with your words and ideas. A big, warm smile in the introduction, when establishing common ground with the audience, never hurt a speaker yet. On your more serious points, you can sneer, scowl, shake and bob your head, and so on. Now, I realize that a major concern of the younger generation is to appear "cool," but audiences still appreciate a speaker who can evoke in them varying emotional responses with language and appearance, including apt facial expressions.

Gestures are used by normal speakers to emphasize or express feelings. Good speakers' gestures add to their intellectual and emotional meanings, rather than detracting from them. As Eisenson *et al.* point out in their *Psychology of Communication:*

> The speaker's gestures, like his words, are derived from the speech community and should reflect this influence. Though the gestures conform to the culture, they, again like the specific selection of his words, also express individuality. The visible compo-

nents of speech are produced and controlled by the individual speaker, and so they become his gestures.

The well adjusting person shows no concern about his gestures unless he finds that they are giving the listener–observer cause for concern. He does not inhibit gestures that will out, nor does he consciously and belatedly produce a gesture past its time to be out. The well adjusting speaker is aware, but without anxiety, that his movements have meaning, but he does not feel impelled to hasten to a psychotherapist to find out just what his last eye-twitch meant. On the other hand, the person who wishes to maintain himself as well adjusting, will seek counsel if he discovers that he has a re-current tic-like movement that is produced in repeated situations, or with a given person or persons, or in a particular place.[2]

As "Master" in the Time/Life film on making a more effec-tive speech says about gesturing, "Don't do unless you feel it."

Leadership

One way to think of public speaking is as a leader–follower situ-ation. You, the speaker, are the leader. The audience members are the followers. You are the expert on your topic, not the audi-ence. You, not one of them, have been chosen (or you chose) to speak on this topic. You are the one who is supposed to *lead them* to the understanding of new information, to acquire different at-titudes, or to take some action. Therefore you must take charge and *be* the leader; to do that you must *act* like a leader.

You must begin before your speech actually starts. Are you to be introduced by a master of ceremonies or a toastmaster? Then sit alertly and listen to that introduction. It might contain some-thing you can adapt to; it might provide you with an opening to demonstrate your versatility, your alertness of mind. Recently I was introduced as a banquet speaker by a friend who lavished a great deal of praise on my previous accomplishments. After tak-ing the rostrum, I pointed out that my friend had said so many nice, flattering things about me that I had begun to say to myself,

[2] Jon Eisenson, J. Jeffery Auer, and John V. Irvin, *The Psychology of Communica-tion* (New York: Appleton-Century-Crofts, Inc., 1963), p. 343. Reprinted here by permis-sion of Harcourt, Brace, and Jovanovich, Inc.

"Either I'm a lot better than I thought, or else I am *dead.*" It went over nicely.

Whether you have been introduced or your name has merely been called as "the next speaker," you must now begin to *demonstrate leadership.* Stride purposefully and surely to the lectern; don't drag yourself up there as if you were going to your execution. Smile. Look as if you're about to really enjoy yourself.

Once you get to the lectern, you should express to the audience, nonverbally, that you are looking forward eagerly to beginning your talk—but not before you are satisfied that it will begin on its very best legs. Do not hurry. Place your notes or other materials and arrange them as you want them. Then look up and over the entire audience for several moments before you begin speaking. Smile, perhaps. This tells the audience, "Here I am up here; there you are down there. When I am sure you are all attentive, I shall begin." You are establishing yourself as the temporary leader of this group.

End your speech strongly. Make sure you have a strong tag line. Then hit it with a strong downward inflection: ". . . and so let me just repeat that if we can adopt this plan soon enough, we will be able to provide security for ourselves, our children, and our nation." Do not continue, then, with "Thank you." That stale bromide says, "This sure has been a dull, uninspiring job on my part, but thanks a lot for your boundless patience for sitting through this claptrap." That's not *leadership!* Hit that "our *nation,*" and *stop.* Begin picking up your notes. Applaud yourself if the audience does not.

"Ok," you say, "that's fine for you, an experienced pro, to say that—but what about us poor scared novices? How the heck are we going to exude leadership with our knees knocking and our cerebral cortex fading into oblivion?" And you have every right to ask just that.

My answer is that you have to make the personal decision to do it. You have to use the so-called James–Lange theory of emotion and decide to act and behave like a leader; because if you will act and behave like a leader, you will *feel* like a leader. If you continually act and behave like a loser, that's what you will ever be.

I admit to being greatly influenced by Dr. Harold Greenwald's *Direct Decision Therapy*. He says we all make decisions that make us what we are, and we stick with these decisions as long as they continue to provide us with payoffs. A man might be depressed, for instance. By being depressed all the time, this man is constantly reassured and paid attention by friends and family; normal demands are not made of him. He is looked after; his needs are met by his fellows.

If being depressed ceases to reap rewards (let's say his friends and family get fed up and decide to ignore this pain in the tail), the guy will probably decide to change. Being depressed all the time is no fun when you have to do it all by yourself. Dr. Greenwald would tell him, once he had decided to change, to start practicing smiling all the time; to make deliberate efforts to be cheerful and friendly; to pat little kids on the head and speak nicely to stray dogs. This behavior becomes infectious, and soon, presto, our depressed dullard is a Cheerful Charlie!

When Franklin D. Roosevelt was struck down by polio, his political ambitions were only delayed, not killed. In order to keep his name before the public, he asked his wife, Eleanor, to fill in for him on his extensive public-speaking schedule.

Eleanor, a private and shy person, was terrified of taking on those speaking engagements. But out of fierce loyalty to her husband, she hitched up what courage she could manage and gave it the good try. She was not entirely successful at first, but she kept doggedly working at it. And she gradually got better and better. She is now remembered as one of our century's top public-speaking figures, among other things. She is quoted in my *Crown Treasury of Relevant Quotations* as having said or written, "I believe that anyone can conquer fear by doing the things he fears to do, provided he keeps doing them until he gets a record of successful experiences behind him."

To be a really successful public speaker, then, you have to make the decision to try leadership. If this decision is too much for you, do not expect success as a public speaker.

Artifactual Communication

We must touch on one other aspect of nonverbal communication that goes along with vocal and visible delivery: it is currently called *artifactual communication,* meaning how you look and dress.

Ordinarily, as a speaker, you should make sure your dress and appearance fit within the norms suitable to the audience to whom you will speak. If it is a formal affair, dress formally. For less formal situations, dress less formally. What you need to remember is that just as in vocal or visual delivery, your artifactual communication—what you communicate by how you look—should not interfere with the audience's understanding and appreciation of what you have to say. Avoid any extreme of dress or grooming that is not consonant with your message.

And remember, as pointed out above, that how you look is going to communicate something to your audience whether you want it to or not. And what is communicated may not be what you expected. A young man with long, unkempt hair may think he is communicating, "I am a fiercely independent thinker," when the audience may be receiving the message, "I am a bum and I don't give a hang that you think so." The young woman wearing ragged jeans, shower clogs, and no makeup may have the same message inconsistency.

Finally, let's take up some final don'ts.

1. Don't scratch your ear, your nose, your stomach, or anything else.

2. Don't put your hands in your pockets; especially, do not put your hand in your pocket and jiggle your keys!

3. Don't play with anything in your hands while talking, whether it be a pencil, a visual aid to be used later, or three steel balls (à la Captain Queeg). That's a sure sign of speaking immaturity.

4. Do not ever take a watch out of your pocket, look at it searchingly, and then elaborately lay it down before you. I have never yet seen a speaker end his speech on time who did so.

5. Don't fiddle with your wardrobe. Don't twist buttons or rings, smooth lapels, or tug on vests.

6. Don't constantly push or throw your hair back out of your eyes. If you have to do that too often, you apparently have to look down at the lectern too much. Learn your speech better, and nail stray locks with some hairspray. Or get a haircut (I admit to prejudice here—I wear a crewcut, short, so have not had to comb my hair since 1945).

7. Don't use the lectern to hold yourself up.

8. Don't take your glasses off and put them back on repeatedly "for effect." If you have a visual problem that requires that for speaking, get different glasses—bifocals, if necessary. You don't want the audience counting the number of times you remove your glasses instead of listening to what you have to say.

9. Don't use a pointer to fence with the front-row listeners.

8

Teach People Something Useful: Speak to Inform

Speeches that inform teach. To *teach* means to cause new information or knowledge to become learned. Elemental? Yes, but you would be surprised at how many speeches I have heard that were supposed to be "speeches to inform" but were not. Each of those alleged speeches to inform did not inform for one or more of the following reasons:

1. *Information altitude: technical words and jargon.* To convey meaning, a word or statement must stir up in the minds of the audience the same picture that was in the mind of the speaker. I recently heard a student speak on the technicalities of igniting a hydrogen bomb. His multisyllabic vocabulary and nuclear shorthand completely baffled the audience.

2. *Information overkill.* Some speakers try to cover too much ground in a short speech, completely bewildering the audience. Ever try to teach an audience in six minutes how to play backgammon? or bridge? or poker? It cannot be done. But there are folks who will try!

3. *Information undershoot.* To inform, you must provide new information; do nothing but repeat trivia the audience already knows, and you bore. Can you imagine a college student speaking to other college students on "How to Write a Check on Your Bank Account"? It happened in my class in the winter quarter of 1980. I also once had a college student speak on how to operate three kinds of can openers, one of which was the traditional "church key" to open beer cans. Unbelievable.

4. *Information scattershot.* Quickly, now: recite the Ten Commandments. You cannot? You have been hearing or reading them all your life, off and on, and you *still* can't remember all of them? Well, then, how about if I gave you a short speech on "Ten Things to Remember When _____ing." How many of *them* would you remember right after the speech? How about next week? How many speeches have you heard where the speaker wanted you to remember "ten things," or twelve principles, or nine places to go? You were being asked to do something your nervous system is not designed for.

5. *Information apathy.* Do people go around all day, constantly hungering and thirsting for information? Do people generally suffer from perpetual curiosity about everything and anything? Of course not. Do you? Most people consider learning labor— it's associated with school "work." So when you get up to speak about shoes or ships or sealing wax, do you expect your audi-

ence to lap up ravenously every crumb of information you toss them? Do so, and you will flop. But all too often, speakers seem to take the podium with just this attitude.

How do you avoid these disasters? Let's take them in order.

1. Avoid technical words and/or jargon. Do not let those specialized words from your vocabulary slip out; and simple common sense (*if you will call on it*) will tell you what technical words you cannot use with clear meaning. Of course, if, as suggested in Chapter 2, you TRY THE SPEECH OUT BEFOREHAND on some people comparable to your audience and get their reactions, you will find out very quickly what jargon is indecipherable.

2 and 3. Information overkill and undershoot can be overcome only with some sensible audience analysis. The most important thing to know about an audience for a speech to inform is how much they already know. You must, then, avoid both speaking over their heads and talking down to them.

It is sometimes very difficult to find out an audience's information level, but maturity and experience in audience analysis usually improve this ability. Generally, it is a good idea to assume that the audience has some knowledge, but not as much as you have, so speak on a kind of middle ground. And leave time for lots of questions, to find out firsthand the knowledge level of the audience.

It would be even better to find some representative members of the group, question them about their information level on your topic, and then generalize it to the entire audience. Or you can talk to the leaders of the organization you're to speak to, for instance; they will be able to give you a pretty accurate profile of the group's knowledge of your topic.

Of course, if you are a student and speaking to students, you ought to be able to estimate pretty well how much they already know about your subject. After all, you yourself will be an "expert student"!

4. Scattershot can be overcome in a couple of ways.

First of all, remember that the human nervous system resembles an electronic computer in some ways, but not in others. Both take in input, store it, and then reproduce it, on call, as output.

The difference is that *every bit* of information fed properly into a computer registers and is stored; and each computer can store millions of such bits of information and reproduce them, every one if necessary. But human beings are hard-pressed to remember seven numerical digits told them long enough to dial the telephone.

Another difference is that computers remember bits of information regardless of whether those bits are related; humans remember better when information is related and interrelated. Which is easiest for *you* to remember of the following?

```
2965   5802   4624   8695   8853
```

or

```
1776   1864   1898   1914   1941?
```

The point? If your speech depends for its effectiveness on the audience's remembering a long string of facts, or points, or ideas, you are doomed to failure. The nervous system can't absorb a lot of detail, store it, and then reproduce it. You have to (1) limit the information you present orally and (2) organize the information around just two or three or four *main* points, or generalizations, which the audience *can* remember.

Let's take an example I like to use a lot.

When I lived in Nebraska, I would get a speech in each class on "Twenty-seven Tips for Wintertime Driving." These tips would be dutifully "listed" orally by the speaker with the barest introduction and conclusion for bookends. Who can remember twenty-seven tips?

The speech content would be much more memorable if organized around three guiding principles that any numskull driver could remember who has lived through a Nebraska winter:

    I. Winter is hard on automobiles, so extra care is necessary to keep your car in shape.
       A. Tip
       B. Tip, etc.

    II. Winter conditions slow you down, so you need to provide more time to get where you're going.
      A. Tip
      B. Tip, etc.
    III. Sudden winter storms on the plains and ordinary unexpected snows in town mean you need to carry some basic equipment in your trunk.
      A. Tip
      B. Tip, etc.

There is one other thing you can do if you think your audience needs lots of details. Make your "list," or "diagram," or "outline" in writing. Duplicate it and hand it out. A student of mine gave a speech on the town's "drinking problem," the "problem" being that few people knew which bars and clubs had happy hours and other bargains on which nights and at what times. So he spoke on that and then handed out to the audience the list of watering spots and their schedules of drinking bargains. When I speak on "The Phylogenetic Theory of Humor Development," I hand out a one-page diagram of humor's "family tree" so that people can follow along with me easily.

And again, if you try out your speech beforehand on a representative rehearsal audience, you will find quickly enough from their feedback whether you are guilty of information overkill, undershoot, or scattershot.

5. *Information apathy* may be a misnomer. I used the term only to maintain parallel structure through my list of five reasons for failure.

It *is* true that ordinarily, few people go around with an insatiable need for any and all information they can clamp their nervous systems onto. Therefore you may wonder why anyone would be the least bit interested in hearing about *your* topic.

An expert on the listening process once stated that "There are no uninteresting topics, only uninterested listeners." What you must do, then, is to make your potentially uninterested listeners into people definitely interested in your topic. It is your job as speaker to ensure that your speech will *create* and *sustain* interest. Let's face it: any fairly literate human being can look up a bunch of information and say it aloud to an audience. But it will take some skill and work to make that information *palatable* to the audience. You must make your audience *want* to learn your information, and in three basic ways.

First, you adapt your information to what you know or can find out about the interests your audience members already have. What does that mean? Let me give you some examples.

Having written a book on humor,[1] I am considered an expert on this topic. As such, I get invitations to speak from all kinds of organizations. I find out the dominant interests of the group to whom I will be speaking and tailor my speech to those interests.

When asked to speak at a luncheon peopled by psychologists and psychiatrists from our health service, I inquired of their program chairman why these folks met biweekly. He told me they were held together by a mutual interest in mental health. So my topic for the luncheon speech became "Mental Health and the Psychology of Humor." A group of pharmacy professors and graduate students invited me to speak to their biweekly seminar on "improving teaching." I spoke on "Teaching with Wit and Humor," reviewing with them the research findings on the topic, and illustrating one concept I personally teach with humor: "The Role of Selective Perception in the Communication Process." This latter is a slide-and-talk show using mostly "Beetle Bailey" and "Family Circus" cartoons.

Invited to speak to a home economics faculty–student–alumni banquet whose weekend convocation was based on the theme of "Handling Stress in Modern America," I spoke on "The Sense of Humor and Stress." For a Rotary Club meeting I spoke on "Laughter: The International Language," because Rotarians are notoriously internationally minded (they sponsor international student exchanges and so on). For the Georgia Authors' Club, I chose for my topic "The Origin and Evolution of Humor." I assumed that authors would be interested in any aspect of humor, but especially in those features that help to explain why people are what they are and behave as they do.

Another commonsense suggestion: assume you are going to be a member of your own audience and ask yourself, "What would *I* like to hear regarding this topic that would be useful to *me?*"

---

[1] Charles R. Gruner, *Understanding Laughter: The Workings of Wit and Humor.* Chicago: Nelson-Hall, 1978.

I like to call this process of audience analysis and self-questioning in order to decide on how to tailor your speech to a specific audience "finding the right psychological hook on which to hang your speech." It takes a little time, thought, and maybe even some ingenuity. But if you are to become a *successful* public speaker, you need to make the effort to find that hook. And not only must you find that hook, you must *use* it in the introduction of your speech to "hook" the audience. This is the rationale for audience interest first mentioned early in Chapter 5. Example:

> I'm sure that each of you has been dazzled and amazed at least once by the illusions of a professional magician. You see that ball, or that veil, or that rabbit appear from seemingly nowhere, and you ask, "How in the world did he do *that?*" Right? Well, today I am going to give away part of the secret. I'm going to show you how a stage magician uses *misdirection* to trick an audience.

A second major way of keeping an audience interested is to keep your speech tightly *organized*. As emphasized in Chapter 5, organized material is better remembered than unorganized material. And if your audience can follow your points as parts of a perceived logical whole, they *learn;* as they learn, they become increasingly pleased with the whole process. They begin to share your mastery of the topic. And for most people, this "Ahha!" experience can be quite exhilarating. This is the "Oh, I *understand* now!" reaction.

A third technique is to use in your speech content, style, and delivery the various factors known about human attention. These factors, which automatically impel the human nervous system to attend, can make a so-so recitation of facts a compelling experience. Let's examine each briefly.

Factors of Attention

Animation, of course, is absolutely vital for holding your audience's attention. This point was underscored in Chapter 7 on delivery. You must radiate alertness and interest in your audience through vocal inflection, apt facial expressions, movement, and gestures. Remember, through empathy your audience will reflect whatever amount of alertness and interest you yourself manifest. So try to be the absolute antithesis of the hypnotist, who asks the subject to stare at the unmoving flame of a single candle (or some other monotonous nonstimulus) while intoning evenly, "You are growing sleepy . . . sooo sleepy."

Vitalness in a speech begins with your very first words—in your introduction—when you utilize your "hook" to team up your topic with what is *vital* to your audience. It must continue throughout your speech, or the audience is likely to ask itself, "Why am I being told this? Why do I need to know it?"

Ever ask yourself that question—for instance, in school? "Why do I have to learn this? What good is this required course gonna do me when I get out of school?" If so, you have questioned the vitalness of what you were supposed to be learning— and you probably did not learn it very well. So keep up that audience interest by sprinkling through your speech such comments as:

> And here's another way to *really* save some money . . .
>
> If you *really* want to lose weight, listen to this suggestion . . .
>
> If you want to absolutely amaze your friends with your knowledge of _____, just listen to this . . .
>
> Next I want to explain to you a very simple way to improve your grades with almost no extra effort . . .
>
> Of course, I know that we all need to save gasoline. It's getting scarcer and more and more expensive. Here are three simple techniques for cutting down on your trips to the service station . . .

Familiarity compels interest because, as Joseph Jastrow has said, man is more analogical than logical. Being able to relate something new and strange to something old and familiar is reassuring. While I was explaining to some graduate students some basic points about FORTRAN, a language with which we communicate with computers, one student's quizzical frown turned suddenly into a smile of recognition: "Why, what you are teaching us is just the basic grammar of FORTRAN, isn't it!"

Audience members also like to hear a speaker mention a familiar fact, name, place, or date; the experience is not unlike that of seeing a suddenly familiar face from home while visiting a strange city. A colleague of mine at the University of Nebraska was popular as a high school commencement speaker around the state. Before journeying to some small Nebraska hamlet to commemorate the high school graduation, he would spend some time reading that town's local papers in the state's archives at the university in Lincoln. He was then able to stud his speech with familiar tidbits like "Now last January, when your basketball team's school bus got stuck in the snow on the way to Kearney . . ."

Novelty, the antithesis of familiarity, is also its counterpart in that it holds attention as well. Perhaps the most overused but effective word in sales and advertising is "New!" (and now, "New and Improved!"). Unusual nomenclature, unusual facts, and intriguing new combinations of information surprise and delight. My favorite columnist, Sydney J. Harris, turns out five columns per week, and one or two of them weekly is composed of unusual and interesting "new" facts he has found while looking up something else. He has assembled enough of them to comprise an entire book (*Would You Believe?*), from which we can learn such things as that Louis Pasteur had such a morbid fear of germs and dirt that he avoided shaking people's hands; also, that Berengaria, a queen of England (wife of Richard I), never once set foot in England. Any such unusual facts or illustrations you can find for your speech will perk up your audience's attention level.

Conflict holds attention well but is easier to portray in a persuasive than in an informative speech. However, some speeches to inform can be organized in a kind of problem–solution order that will generate the kind of conflict that arrests the audience's attention. For instance:

   I. Hemophilia is a dread disease that kills 85 percent of its victims.
     A. Causes . . .
     B. Effects . . .
  II. Medical science is making inroads on ways to treat hemophilia.

A speaker can utilize suspense by withholding the most important points of the speech until near the end. It can also be used in short illustrations and examples, or even at the level of the *sentence* on what are called *periodic sentences,* those with the most important information at or near the end. Contrast the following two statements:

> My wallet was picked from my pocket last December while I rode the subway from Forty-second Street to Seventieth.
>
> Last December, while riding the subway from Forty-second Street to Seventieth, I suddenly discovered that my wallet had been picked from my pocket.

Concreteness of language has already been discussed in Chapter 6 as making for greater clarity and vividness. Suffice it to say here that it also holds interest better than its opposite, abstractness. Concrete, specific language by the speaker allows the listeners mental economy by making it easy for them. Concrete language also stirs up in the audience's minds a more exact picture of what the speaker had in mind. Contrast the following:

Abstract	*Concrete*
He's middle-aged.	He'll be fifty-one in October.
It's a long way from here.	It is five hours by auto.
She went to the office.	She caught the bus to the office.
He's pretty sick.	He has pneumonia and is listed in "fair" condition.

Humor has been found by experimental studies (mine) to add interest to a speech that is not very interesting to begin with; however, if a speech already has a great many other interest factors in it, humor seems to add no further interest. However, common sense tells us that if we expect a speaker to entertain us with humor while we are listening to the information (or the persuasion), we will listen with a bit more attention than usual. And the expectation of being entertained will draw an audience *to* the speaker. For example, consider Dick Gregory, comedian, author, lecturer, and civil rights activist. He currently (1981) speaks professionally only on college campuses. He has a fascinating blend of humor, wit, and civil rights message, and he draws large, well-paying crowds.

I want to make one point before leaving humor. It is not necessary to tell jokes in your speeches. If you can do it well and the humor "fits in" without demeaning, embarrassing, or insulting anyone, it probably will do no harm. But don't think that you must always begin with a good opening joke.

Types of Speeches to Inform

Speeches to inform can probably best be cataloged by type of subject matter. Let us consider a few, some possible topics for each, and ways in which they can best be organized.

Processes.   Many speeches to inform, especially of the classroom variety, are on some process, or "how to do it" or "how something works." Examples of topics for such speeches are the following:

The Triple Option Play in Football	Sewing on a Button
Putting in Golf	How a Nuclear Generator Works
Cooking Crepes	How Marshes Promote Good Ecology
Soil Testing	A Balanced Diet
Federal Pesticide Controls	CPR (Coronary Pulmonary Resuscitation)
The Heimlich Maneuver	Making Your Own Beer Pretzels

Most speeches on "how to do it" would take a chronological pattern:

    I. The first major step is to . . .
   II. The second major step is to . . .
  III. Finally, you must . . .

Some topics are best handled with a topical arrangement:

    I. Marshes are important to wildlife because . . .
   II. Marshes are valuable for soil ecology in that they . . .
  III. Marshes benefit us by . . .

Products or Discoveries.   Do you know of a new product that is due on the market soon? Or a new medical or other scientific discovery not well-known already? A speech on it could be highly useful to your audience. This area would include such topics as

The New "Natural" Pesticides	"Silverless" Photographic Film
The New Laser Operation for Eliminating "Port Wine" Birthmarks	The Latest in SCUBA Gear
Realistic Substitutes for Steak	Gasohol
A Practical Windmill for Your Home	Insects as Human Food
New Hope for Cancer Patients	A New Plastic Coating for Your Car
Methane Gas from Peat	The Conquest of Smallpox

Many of these topics could be handled in a topical order. Others could be handled in a problem–solution order:

    I. Port wine birthmarks, especially on the face, have been an aesthetic embarrassment for many . . .
   II. A new process, using lasers, eliminates port wine birthmarks quickly and painlessly . . .
  III. The new technique is practical and not as expensive as you might think . . .

Other topics, to show how they came into being, might follow the chronological pattern.

Concepts or Ideas.   Abstract ideas or concepts that may not be easily or universally understood might make excellent topics for a speech to inform, such as:

Wit Versus Humor	Comedy Versus Farce
"Classic" Versus "Old Standard"	Legal Sense of "Double Jeopardy"
The Statute of Limitations	Freedom Versus Responsibility
What Is a "Scholar"?	Leadership Versus Management
The Entrepreneur in America	A Managed Economy
Logotherapy (or Any Other System of Psychotherapy)	Adam Smith's "Capitalism"

Speeches on many topics such as these might be "one-point speeches," in that there would be only one main point plus its explanation. Others would probably fit the topical mode of arrangement best.

People or Places. Unusual information about a person or a place can make an interesting speech. However, the danger here is coming up with a speech that merely interests or entertains without providing information that is truly useful in either a practical or an intellectual sense. For instance, I recently heard a student speech on George Washington that emphasized facts of his life to show that he was not at all the "perfect" American so often depicted in third grade (for instance, we learned that the Father of Our Country was so fearful of being buried alive that he specified an unusually long time between pronouncement of death and interment).

We might also make speeches to inform on *groups* of people, or organizations, such as the UN General Assembly, the Mormon Church, Rotary International, or the "Moonie" movement.

Oral Reports

A special form of the speech to inform is the oral report, and I feel it deserves special handling because you are quite apt to have to make one or more of these during your life. Oral reports are distinguished by four characteristics:

1. The reporter has usually been assigned the duty of making the report.

2. The audience (or part of it) has usually assigned the report and must act upon it's contents.

3. The report's contents are usually technical and specialized, based on some original investigation by the reporter and/or others.

4. The report has its own unique pattern of arrangement.

Probably the most usual use of the oral report is that of the chairperson of an *ad hoc* (temporary) committee to the parent group that assigned the committee a particular task. The report is composed of the following: the introduction, a description of operational processes, the findings, and the recommendation(s).

Let me exemplify by briefly outlining the report of Mrs. Wilma Braun to the Board of Directors of the Northeast Georgia Girl Scout Council. Her committee was responsible for screening applicants for a new executive director for the council.

Introduction. Good evening. Your committee, composed of _____, has worked hard, and we think we have a fine candidate for your approval.

Operational Processes. Our committee met _____ times. We set the following criteria for evaluating the applicants: _____, _____, _____, and _____.

We advertised locally, regionally, and nationally in GSA publication and local papers, such as _____.

We eventually received twenty-one applications.

We narrowed these down to two; these applicants were brought in for visits and interviews.

We felt that both were highly qualified for the position, but we thought one best fit our needs for growth and vigor.

Findings. We therefore concluded that the best candidate for the job of executive director was Paula Christy Heighton. We asked her if she would accept the job if this board ratified our choice. She said she would.

Recommendation. Our committee therefore unanimously asks the board to ratify the appointment of Paula Christy Heighton as executive director of the Northeast Georgia Girl Scout Council.

Because our country is one run by committees, there is a good chance you will make a report like this one sometime before you die. But note that the above organizational format is the same used by the scientist for making reports on scientific discoveries:

Introduction. A search and review of available research studies show that Glop produces Gog when stirred in the presence of Goo; however, there is no evidence that it has ever produced Gog when stirred in the presence of Geeg. The study reported here hypothesized that Glop would produce Gog when stirred in the presence of Geeg, but only under certain circumstances of light and temperature.

Operational Processes. Light and temperature were controlled by. _____. The Glop-stirring was accomplished with a GTXM412 Glop-Stirrer manufactured by the Diamond X company. Presence of Geeg in the experimental apparatus was limited to _____. Gog production was checked for with a Mathis Gogometer with a sensitivity range of _____.

Findings. Traces of Gog were found when Glop was stirred at _____ rpm under light and temperature intensities of _____ and _____, but only when Geeg was present in amounts of _____ or greater.

Recommendations. It seems unlikely that stirring Glop in the presence of Geeg will become a commercially viable method of producing Gog.

Because an oral report may require a recommendation, it might seem more classifiable as a speech to persuade. However, the speaker might leave the recommendation out and wait for a motion from the floor or another officer. Also, the recommendation must be based on a very solid base of information explained in the "operational processes" section, because that is where most of the speech content will be. After all, it tells how the problem was handled and how the results were achieved; and how information is gained is quite often more important than the information itself. For instance, suppose I told you that I had done a survey, and that two out of three surveyed said they thought taxes should be raised by at least 25 percent. Wouldn't you be interested in how many and what kind of people I had talked to?

9

Rearrange Some Prejudices: Speak to Persuade

When you speak to persuade, you provide your listeners with information, but not just for the sake of teaching them that information. The purpose of the speech to persuade is to provide not only information but a motivation to change or to affirm audience thinking or behavior. You must therefore concentrate on the thinking or behavior you desire from the audience.

Let us be very candid about *how* people think and behave.

People think and behave, by and large, just the way they *want* to. Put another way, people choose to believe and to do what pleases them.

Let us consider thinking, or the operation of attitudes, first.

Each of us may have an attitude toward war, God, liver and onions, politics, motherhood, "the Arabs," television, or rock music. And our attitude toward any one of those things will shape and control how we think and behave concerning it. If our attitude *pleases* us, we will continue to hold that attitude. Specifically, we will continue to hold onto an attitude to the extent it provides one or more of the following:

1. Satisfaction of our basic physical needs, including food, shelter, and sex.

2. A feeling of mastery over our environment, or part of it.

3. A sense of success in our vocation and/or avocation.

4. Gratification of our need to be loved and wanted.

5. Successful avoidance of worry and anxiety, and the attainment of peace of mind.

6. Adventure and new experience.

Yes, people do believe what pleases them. Why in the world else would a substantial percentage of Americans today still believe that America has *not* put men on the moon and brought them back safely? It is because they refuse to believe the newspaper and magazine reports; they explain that those amazing moon films on television are special-effects propaganda manufactured by our government!

And people *do* what pleases them, too. Oh, sure, there are some things we *have* to do, and we *do* them because we have to

126

do them. We have to get up in the morning; we have to wear clothes (most of the time); we have to obey the traffic laws (again, most of the time); we have to go to school a minimum amount of time; and we have to be nice to people we detest. But even things that we have to do are usually things we agree are things we ought to do. After all, for example, if a law is passed that does not have substantial popular support, it fails. The Nineteenth Amendment to the U.S. Constitution against drinking collapsed because of enforceability problems: you cannot arrest a majority of the citizens! And I just recently took a long auto trip, obeying pretty well the present speed limit of 55 mph. I was passed a great deal, but I passed few other vehicles. And I saw not one car ticketed for speeding.

That people do and believe what they want to is the single most important fact that you as a would-be persuader must know and adhere to. Why? Simple. You must find and articulate in your speech the reasons that your audience *should* want to believe or do as you want them to believe or do. This necessity implies several assumptions.

First, you will have to know the satisfactions to be derived from believing or doing as you ask. This *should* be ridiculously simple. You already believe in your idea or already do what you are going to urge others to do. So you ought to be able to figure out why *you* believe or do it! (And if you cannot figure out why you believe or do something, you're in trouble—and would have difficulty persuading anyone else on that topic.)

Second, you will need to analyze your audience to find out why they do not already believe or do what you want them to. Are they basically ignorant of your topic? Then maybe just an information-based approach is all that is needed. Are they informed but apathetic? Then your problem is to provide more motivation to believe or act. Are they already basically in agreement with you? Then a pep-talk approach might suffice. Are they actively opposed to your point? Then you know you will need a great many compelling arguments backed by solid evidence *plus* strong, impelling motives for them to believe or act as you wish them to.

Third, if you find that your audience holds attitudes and opinions quite different from your own, you must avoid offense on these deep-seated, emotional feelings. Otherwise the audience is likely to reject you; and if they do, they also reject your ideas. Several years ago, the Mountain Bell Telephone System broadcast the following radio advertisement for its services. It is printed here by permission of Mountain Bell.

> OPERATOR: I *will* place that call for you, if you wish, but it's much cheaper if you dial direct.
>
> MAN: Oh, well, that's the point. I want her to know that I'm spending a lot of money on her.
>
> OPERATOR: Oh, I understand. Certainly, sir. One moment. (Buzz—Buzz)
>
> WOMAN: Hello.
>
> OPERATOR: Miss Lucinda Jacobson, please.
>
> WOMAN: Speaking.
>
> OPERATOR: I have a call for you placed the *more expensive* way—through an operator. It was not dialed direct. Is that OK, Sir?
>
> MAN: That's fine.—Hi, Cindy, this is Rocky. How are you?
>
> WOMAN: You *fool!*

Obviously, Rocky did not correctly analyze his audience, Cindy. To be a successful persuader, then, you must analyze your audience thoroughly, *Work hard* (see Chapter 1), and have a proven plan or strategy for presenting your proposal. We now turn to the plan or strategy that has been the most successful in our free society. Alan H. Monroe, late of Purdue University, formulated it and popularized it as the "motivated sequence."

The Motivated Sequence

Professor Monroe's plan is a series of five chronological steps that follow psychologically the stages by which human beings learn and become motivated to adopt an attitude or a plan of action. Briefly it involves:

1. Getting the *attention* of the audience focused, bolted onto your topic.

2. Demonstrating to them that some *need* in their lives exists.

3. Showing that your solution will directly lead to the *satisfaction* of that need.

4. Creating in their minds' eyes a *visualization* of the resulting doom that will descend if your solution is not adopted, and/or picturing for them the hope, joy, and happiness they can expect if your solution is adopted.

5. Calling them successfully to take *action* on your proposal.

These five steps, naturally, are called the *attention, need, satisfaction, visualization,* and *action* steps. Let us consider each in detail.

Attention Step.   This is your introduction, and it must cross what has been called the *interest deadline* quickly. Of course, when you get up to speak, you may not have to get the audience's *attention,* exactly. After all, you'll be standing up in front of them; they will be seated facing you; they are expecting a speech from you. You will have their general attention. But you still must focus that attention immediately on your topic through one or more of the interest factors taken up in the preceding chapter.

For the professional persuader, out in the field (that is, the "real world"), capturing attention in the very first moment of contact is absolutely imperative; the politician, the sales representative, and the advertiser must open with a compelling introduction. For instance, the advertiser places an ad in a magazine. That ad must freeze to itself the reader, who is riffling through the pages to get to the stories and cartoons; that reader's attention must be captured in the blink of an eye. How does it happen? With a full-color picture of a handsome man or woman or both (sex), an appetizing food, a cute baby or puppy—maybe white space, perhaps bold headlines of vital importance to the target audience ("Melt off Body Fat without Dieting"), and so on. The TV commercial might make use of any of the above, with the added advantage of loud sound (commercials are recorded louder) and animated movement. If the TV ad doesn't grab you instantly, you might head for the bathroom or the refrigerator, and the advertiser has spent thousands of dollars for nothing, as far as you are concerned.

Near the end of the attention step, you should present your thesis, at least in general terms. For instance,

> . . . and that's my topic today. I am going to try to get you to take up bicycling,

can be more generally introduced as:

> . . . and so my topic today is to try to get you to adopt a new kind of transportation that is fun, healthy, and inexpensive, and that consumes no fossil fuels.

Need Step.   Depending on the kind of topic you have, your need step should do one of two things: (1) present the audience with a particular problem that cries out for a solution, or (2) kindle an unfulfilled desire. Let us go through the stages of the need step, illustrating them briefly with two topics: (1) the problem of a deteriorating municipal water purification plant and (2) the desire to get out into the great outdoors by backpacking.

First, you need a definite, concise *statement* of the problem (or desire) that the audience can comprehend in definite, concrete terms: (1) "Our city faces a severe shortage of drinking water within the next ten years because of a deteriorating water plant built in 1927." (2) "We young and affluent Americans today are becoming a bunch of overweight, out-of-shape, indoor dwellers, missing out on the greatest gifts of nature."

Next, *illustrate* the problem, giving one or more detailed examples that can help make the problem (or desire) concrete in the minds of the audience: (1) "Just last year Jefferson City was having the same problems that we will soon be having. Just last November they were rationing water." (2) "Until three years ago, I was 20 pounds overweight. Walking up two flights of stairs winded me. I found that I was addicted to sitting before the hypnotic eye of the television set."

The next step could be giving the ramifications of the problem—additional examples, facts, and statistics: (1) "If our growth in population and industry continues for three years at the rate of

the past ten, our needs will outstrip our maximum ability to produce 10.5 million gallons of water per day." (2) "Medical statistics
show that an estimated 34 percent of people fifteen to twenty-six
are at least partly overweight. The latest figures from the old selective service show that over half the young men drafted after
1957 had serious problems of physical conditioning."

The final phase of the need step is utterly crucial: it is called
pointing, and it involves directly relating the need or problem to
the audience who sits before you, not some vague "public." For
if the live audience attending your speech is allowed to say to
itself, "Yeh, sounds pretty bad, but, thank goodness, it isn't *my*
problem," you have lost them: (1) "Without a new water supply
in this town in the next three years, it will soon be *you* for whom
water will be rationed." (2) "Now is the time for *you* to do something about the growing roll around your middle, to break away
from the TV, to get interested in the out-of-doors—while you are
still young and without the responsibilities of starting a career
and raising a family."

Satisfaction Step.   Your need step has made the audience wor-
ried, anxious, and fearful; they are upset. They want to do something. In short, they itch.

You now come to their rescue. You show them how to
scratch. You give them *satisfaction,* in five steps.

A. Again, you clearly *state* the new attitude to adopt or the
action to take. Make perfectly clear what your solution is: (1) "We
must pass in April the new city bond issue for the proposed new
water system." (2) I propose that you *try,* at least, a most satis-
fying form of recreation: backpacking."

B. *Explain.* Make sure your proposal cannot be misunderstood: (1) "What I am asking is for each of us to go to the polls
April 13 and vote 'Yes' for Proposition 2." (2) "I don't mean that
you should run out and spend $400 on equipment and hit the
most rugged section of the Appalachian Trail this weekend. But
you can try it out to see if you like it by renting and borrowing
the minimal equipment and then sample backpacking at a state
park some long weekend."

C. Show how your plan meets and solves the problem: (1)
"The Water Board estimates that the new system that Proposition

2 would provide will supply us with all the water we will need through the year 2050." (2) "Complete backpacking provides lots of fresh air and exercise, ensures a healthful nutrition plan, and gets you out where you can commune with nature."

D. Give your audience a "for instance" or two. Show where your plan has worked before—again, so that they can mentally transform your abstract words into concrete reality: (1) "Proposition 2 would provide us almost the same kind of system that Jefferson City installed. They have a water system *par excellence*. Let me tell you about their . . ." (2) "Until I took up backpacking over two years ago, I was a flabby, pale, TV junkie. Now I weigh fifteen pounds less, feel great, and regularly hike into absolutely beautiful country that fewer than 1 percent of our citizens ever see."

E. The final phase of the satisfaction step is the overcoming of objections. For if a member of the audience walks away saying inwardly, "Yes, it all sounds OK on the surface, *but*. . . ," again you have lost. That member still has doubt, or an objection that is not yet banished. In this step, you must anticipate and forestall any and all objections that might be brought up.

What are the usual general objections? "It takes too much time—or money—or effort; the solution will create other problems; there may be other solutions just as good that the speaker did not mention."

And then, almost every specific proposition will have some specific objections inherent in it. "Buy a Volkswagen" might be resisted because the car is "too small." "Read *Gone with the Wind*" may be countered with "I've already read it" (in which case, you come back with "You get more out of it on the second or third reading").

The importance of overcoming objections cannot be overly stressed. I have, for instance, in my "persuasion file" a sales manual for the sales representatives of a well-known encyclopedia. The manual is primarily a book of rebuttals to expected customer objections. The sales representative memorizes these rebuttals and thus can overcome any objection the hapless customer might manage. For instance, the sales representative knows by heart *six* different rebuttals to the customer objection, "I can't afford it." To the objection, "I want to think it over" (an objection the sales rep must *never* let stand), there are *thirteen* rebuttals! "Our children are too young" can be met with any one of four rebuttals. And the list goes on.

The point? Being prepared to overcome audience objections is absolutely vital. If you do not expect a forum period after your speech, you must handle those expected objections at the end of the satisfaction step of your speech. If you don't, you will fail as badly as the fellow in my class who tried to get us all to spend the summer in Europe. He made it sound like fun, but he never once told us how we could manage the expense. When I asked him why he had not overcome this objection, he replied lamely that he knew Europe would be too expensive for us and so he had not wanted to mention that "negative point."

Visualization Step.   Once you have the audience's attention, created an itch in them, and told them how to scratch it, you may think you are done. But you are not. The scratching may not become a habit. In fact, just *thinking* about the scratching may make them think they have done something about the itch. And some itches disappear in time with no scratching. You must heighten and "emotionalize" their scratching behavior by making the audience *visualize* the future—with and without your solution.

The *negative* method paints for the audience's imagination a dark and disastrous tableau. The *positive* method depicts a bright and happy future of hope and joy. The good speaker combines the two into the "method of contrast."

(1) "Let this bond issue fail in April, and in a few months you might wake up one morning, turn on the spigot to brush your teeth, and get nothing but a gurgle. Turning on the radio to the local news you will find that *your* street will get water on odd-numbered days of the month only. *But* help pass the bond issue next April, and we can look forward to all the sweet, fresh water we will need in our lifetimes. No need to do without watering the parched lawn in August. Have all the water you need for the laundry, the wading pool, the car washing . . ."

(2) "So you can continue your sedentary, indoor life. You

can walk only from your desk to your car to the dining table to the chair before the TV while you work on that heart attack at age forty. Or you can become a backpacker, toughen your legs and body, rejuvenate your heart, and open your senses to the wilderness. Learn what it's like to sleep and wake up by a gurgling mountain stream miles away from the sounds of man-made noise. Discover the thrill of ascending to the valley's rim for a view that you have truly earned, and find that it was worth it . . . "

The visualization step is the one least used and the one used least well by the beginning and younger speaker, and I have often wondered why. If one is highly motivated to convince or actuate an audience, it should be easy to probe one's own mind and conjure up the words for the negative and positive pictures that can be depicted for the audience's future. This step is sometimes even called the *projection step,* because it does just that: it "projects" the audience into the future so that they can see the effects of the adoption or nonadoption of the proffered solution. It might even be possible for the speaker to find actual examples to provide such projection. Here is an example-type visualization step for a speech on "Wear your seat belt" that I used in another book:

(*Negative*) Oh, I know it's easy to make up excuses to not buckle up on every little trip. Well, just keep on making those excuses, and you might have the kind of "minor" accident Walter H. Cameron of Indianapolis had. Forced off the road and into a concrete abutment at twenty-five miles per hour, Mr. Cameron crashed into the steering wheel with the same force as falling two stories. A broken jaw, three fractured ribs, a cracked elbow, and fourteen stitches in the face and neck were the price he paid for a dangling, unused seatbelt.

(*Positive*) But develop the seatbelt habit, and each time you climb behind the wheel the solid, reassuring metal click of your seatbelt reassures you that you are safe—safe from injury, and a safer driver because you have once again reminded yourself that driving is a serious and risky business. As you drive, the gentle tug at your lap will be a constant reminder of your new status as a safety conscious, safer driver, which can become a source of real personal pride.[1]

---

[1] Charles R. Gruner et al., *Speech Communication in Society,* 2nd ed. Boston: Allyn & Bacon, 1977, p. 210. Printed here by permission of Allyn & Bacon.

So find or produce a visualization step for each persuasive speech. It is this step that turns a red slab of dead steer into a sizzling, savory sirloin steak.

Action Step. Some speeches, especially those to actuate or to convince that action must be taken, benefit from a final call to action (as do many advertisements). There are several ways to do this.

A. There is the direct challenge or appeal: "Don't wait until it's too late. Do it now!" "The sale ends Thursday. Come in tomorrow." "Supply is limited. First come, first served."

B. You can summarize or restate your thesis: "And so you see, we simply have to have that new water system. Be sure to get down to the polls April 13 and vote "Yes" on Proposition 2; and take your friends and neighbors with you to vote for *Progress.*"

C. Maybe a stirring quotation is the way to end your speech. "Goethe said it for all of us: 'Nature knows no pause in progress and development, and attaches her curse on all inaction.' "

D. Perhaps an illustration or brief example can best round out your final thought and mobilize your audience: "Seize your opportunities today. Perhaps you heard of the tightwad Frenchman who saved his one rare bottle of fine wine to toast the end of his long life. When his bottle was opened for his deathbed salute, the wine was found to have turned to vinegar. Drink the wine of life while you have it!"

E. Sometimes a statement of personal intent is most apt: "The student union is sponsoring an easy weekend hike from Woody Gap to Neels Gap the last weekend of the month. I'll be there on that trail. Won't you join me?"

There you have it, the motivated sequence. You will remember that back in Chapter 6, a speech exemplifying the use of this process was presented. You might want to review that speech at this time. But the motivated sequence is not used only in speeches; it is used in a variety of persuasive situations. The next time you are watching television, take note of the one-minute dramatized commercials. You may be surprised to find that many of them routinely click their way through the five steps in the motivated sequence. Another way the motivated sequence is used is in a persuasive *campaign* over a longer period of time than a single message.

Persuasive Campaigns

The accomplishing of large persuasive objectives by large teams and concerning various and sundry audience members scattered by location, intelligence level, education, age, and so on must be done over time. This is the persuasive campaign. And the campaign, as it runs for a long period of time, often goes through the five steps, or stages, of the motivated sequence. For instance, let us consider the problem of a relatively unknown candidate for political office, such as a man running for governor.

This candidate's initial problem is that he is not known outside his own hometown. So he launches a campaign to introduce himself to the statewide electorate (attention step). He disseminates his name and picture everywhere. He might have a campaign song written for him and sung constantly over the radio so that people learn to hear and pronounce his name. The next stage of the campaign would probably be to show that the state has problems that are not being solved, and that the problem lies in the state's "leadership." This is the need step.

After the gubernatorial hopeful feels that the electorate knows his name and are aware of the problems of state leadership, he might give a series of speeches on TV and on campaign trips stating how he, as governor, would solve the various state problems (provide "leadership"). This is nothing more than his satisfaction step. He will probably also have to overcome objections in various forums peopled by hecklers and in broadcast press conferences.

Sometime during the campaign, certainly after he has become known around the state and has come to speak on the issues (both problems and solutions), the candidate is nearly bound to concoct a number of brief TV commercial spots and maybe even some live "media events" designed to dramatize his image. The TV spots, for instance, will never argue the issues. Oh, no. They will picture the candidate earnestly listening to the complaints of a few small-town farmers and will depict his glowing countenance (taken from his best side) gazing confidently into the future as he addresses unseen (but certainly heard) huge throngs of avid followers cheering him on to certain victory (the "bandwagon effect"). Toward the end of the commercial, the colors will fade into tints of red, white, and blue, as martial music rises on cue. This is all pure visualization (and you might say pure something else).

The final action step is always there, sometimes in the wings. Always implied is "Vote for me." Toward the end of the campaign, the focus might be put on "getting out the vote."

In summary, in a long campaign the persuasion might follow the motivated sequence steps, each as a stage of the campaign, each with a specific goal, but all of them taken together aiming for a final, general outcome, or ultimate objective. We could map it this way:

Stage 1 (attention step). Specific goal: to get name, face of candidate known.
Technique: make appearances, play "jingle," advertise widely.
Ultimate objective: to elect candidate governor.

Stage 2 (need step). Specific goal: to create dissatisfaction with opposition.
Technique: attack leadership of state, including other candidates.
Ultimate objective: to elect candidate governor.

Stage 3 (satisfaction step). Specific goal: to convince that candidate can solve the problems.
Technique: present platform, views.
Ultimate objective: to elect candidate governor.

Stage 4 (visualization step). Specific goal: to heighten candidate's image as inspirational leader.
Technique: nonargumentative TV spots, personal media appearances.
Ultimate objective: to elect candidate governor.

Stage 5 (action step). Specific goal: to get out the vote.
Technique: stir up the candidate's faithful.
Ultimate objective: to elect candidate governor.

The same kind of five-stage campaign has also been used in many a successful advertising campaign, especially for a new product.

Types of Persuasive Speeches

There are three general types of persuasive speeches, based on specific purposes of the speaker. These are the speeches to convince, to actuate, and to stimulate. Knowing exactly which kind of speech you are to give—based on the specific change you seek from the audience—is of vital importance, for such knowledge will determine how you go about building the speech from the floor up. Let us consider each kind in its turn.

Speeches to Convince.   Speaking to convince is distinguished by two characteristics. First, it argues a controversial proposition, one on which reasonable and informed people will disagree; in fact, the speaker who must convince assumes that at least *some* in the audience will actually be opposed to the thesis of the speech. Second, although some future audience action might be implied (as, in "Gambling is morally wrong"), the audience response sought is not overt action, but the developing or changing or strengthening of an attitude.

Speeches to convince can be easily divided according to what type of proposition each argues. Again, it is important that you recognize early exactly which kind of proposition you are going to be arguing, for again, the kind of proposition you argue will determine how your speech is constructed.

A speech to convince on a proposition of *policy* argues that a particular action should be taken *now* that will determine actions in the *future*. That is why we say that a proposition of policy concerns the future. Some propositions of policy:

Ownership of guns should (not) be controlled and licensed by the government.

The Equal Rights Amendment should (not) be ratified.

The use of marijuana should (not) be decriminalized.

The United States should (not) stop building nuclear generating plants.

The Delaney Clause should (not) be repealed.

The use of Laetrile should (not) be legalized.

Our state should (not) legalize gambling.

The policy speech should follow the steps of the motivated sequence explicitly, even if you are arguing that a policy should *not* be adopted, as in:

> *Attention step:* Voltaire once said that "The art of medicine consists of amusing the patient while nature cures the disease."
>
> *(No) Need step:* We don't need federal health insurance; most Americans are covered by private health insurance, Medicare, Medicaid, group plans, or combinations thereof.
>
> *(No) Satisfaction step:* Even if we did need some federal plan, Senator Kennedy's plan would result in many other problems, such as skyrocketing expense, . . .
>
> *Visualization step:* If Senator Kennedy's plan did pass, imagine yourself paying the taxes to support the boondoggling billions and billions of dollars it will cost. . . . Let's keep our good old freedom of choice to buy the medical protection we feel we need.
>
> *Action step:* So, if your Congressman or Senator seeks your advice on how to vote on federal health insurance, answer "Heck, no, too much dough!" (This step is optional, as it seeks "action.")

Another way to approach the speech's construction is to make each main point answer each of the three "stock issues" of need(?), best solution(?), and practicality(?), which are inherent in any issue of policy:

1. There are (not) problems with the matter of X.
2. The new proposed plan will (not) solve the problems concerned with X.
3. The new plan is (not) the most practical method of solving the *alleged* problem of X.

This type of arrangement, however, is merely the motivated sequence without the "visualization" step (and with "practicality" coming where "objection overcoming" would come). And I think the motivated sequence is best because a speech on policy is enhanced by the visualization step.

The speech to convince on a proposition of *value* is said to concern the *present*. It says, "at *present* we should (not) place *this* value on *that* entity." Some examples of propositions of value are:

> Foreign cars are (not) inherently better made than American cars.
>
> Capital punishment is (not) un-Christian.
>
> The censorship of television is (not) ridiculous.
>
> It is (not) sinful for fire fighters and police officers to strike.
>
> Zero population growth is (not) desirable today.
>
> The U.S. economy is (not) basically a war economy.
>
> Photography is (not) a true art.
>
> Modern art is (not) decadent.
>
> Professional athletes are (not) overpaid.
>
> Increased defense spending is (not) dangerous.

The speech to convince on a proposition of value ordinarily would not use the motivated sequence, because the "stock issues" inherent in such a proposition do not match those of the motivated sequence. Instead, those two stock issues are (1) "The criteria for determining the value of X are _____." (2) "Application of those criteria prove that X fits (does not fit) those criteria." For example:

> I. "Art" can be defined as an activity fitting the following criteria: _____.
>
> II. Photography is an "art" because it fits the criteria by _____ .

The third kind of speech to convince is the one that argues a question of *fact*. This is a speech that argues that a certain cause–effect relationship is true, that some event happened or did not happen a certain way, or that such-and-such exists or exists in a certain way.

Of course, most propositions of fact we would not argue. Why get into a dispute over who won the Most Valuable Player award in the 1974 Super Bowl? Just look it up! However, there are many propositions of fact that are controversial and over which we might argue strenuously:

> Flying saucers are (not) visitors from another planet.
>
> No-fault auto insurance is (not) doing what it was supposed to do.
>
> Lee Harvey Oswald was (not) the lone assassin of President Kennedy.
>
> Air pollution is (not) shortening Americans' lives.
>
> The Bermuda Triangle is (not) the site of the lost city of Atlantis.
>
> Some forms of cancer are (not) caused by viruses.
>
> Large doses of vitamin C are (not) effective in warding off colds.

The speech to convince on a question of fact presents a unique problem to the speaker. There is *no* set of "stock issues" inherent in its organization, as there are with the propositions of policy and value. This means that the speaker must look to the content of the proposition and choose as main ideas those points that must be made in order to achieve the intended purpose. I recommend especially that a speaker with this problem go back and review Chapter 2 before beginning work on a speech to convince on a matter of fact.

I *have a Pet Peeve:* Some people give a sort of "one-issue" speech that is really only one third (or less) of a speech to convince on *policy*. For instance, I might hear a speech in my class on "We need a new energy policy." Or "Federal health insurance will provide us the following benefits." Or another: "We could solve our population explosion by licensing each person at birth to reproduce himself or herself only once." Now, I feel that such speeches are justified if—and only if—they are meant to be one stage of a *campaign*. Otherwise they are cheap shots. Let me explain.

Take the speech on the energy crisis. Here we have *only* the "need step." And isn't it *easy* to show a need? Almost anyone can point to *any* factor of the status quo (which means "the mess we're in now") and find fault, find problems. I personally feel that you should keep silent about problems until you can offer a solution that will *work* and be practical. Otherwise you're like the whining out-of-office political candidate who screams "Something's gotta be done" but has nothing constructive to suggest.

Consider the speech on federal health insurance. Certainly, a multi-billion-dollar program is going to show *some* benefits for *some* people, primarily those who cannot now afford adequate medical care. But as most Americans are covered by private health insurance or social programs such as Medicare and Medicaid, it would be far easier to show a need for a plan limited to helping only the truly needy.

How about the speech on licensing at birth? It correctly implies a need case (we *do* have an exploding population). And it would work, *if* it weren't illegal, unenforceable, and unconstitutional. What would you do if a couple had triplets? Let them keep only the pick of the litter?

Well, anyway, that's my pet peeve. If you're going to argue what is inherently a *policy* position, show a need, a solution, and its practicality. Be fair.

Speeches to Actuate.   The speech to actuate tries to motivate the audience to do something in particular. The subject matter is often not even controversial; in fact, the audience usually already agrees, intellectually, that they should be doing what you urge. Then why aren't they doing it? They lack sufficient motivation. The speaker must *supply* that motivation.

Just about everyone agrees we ought to read more good literature and watch less junk on TV; that we should get more exercise and eat (less of) a more balanced diet; that we should give more to charity; that we should donate our time to worthy causes; that we should give blood to the Red Cross, if able; that we should buy more life insurance and less snack food; and so on. However, we read less and watch more and more TV; we eat more poorly and get less exercise; we find excuses for not doing our best in all these matters. We choose the worse alternative because of our motivations.

The job of the speaker is to find and communicate the personal benefits of choosing the better alternative. The ideal tool for this job is the motivated sequence. Here are some other possible thesis topics for the speech to actuate:

Take up sewing.	Vote in the next election.
Do not swim in the ocean.	Fast one day a week.
Spay your pet.	Subscribe to the Sunday *New York Times*.
Take a course in first aid.	Read *Newsweek* weekly.
Get a yearly physical exam.	Open a holiday savings account.
Bake your own bread.	Take up jogging.
Take up skydiving.	Get flu shots this fall.
Conserve water.	Begin your Chistmas shopping *now*.
Get a CB radio for your car.	Make your next car a _____
Take up photography.	Write or wire your Senator about _____.
Join the Book-of-the-Month Club.	Go to the Town and Gown show.

Speeches to Stimulate.   For most people, the speech to stimulate or *inspire* would be the toughest one in the book to do successfully. For it is on a topic that the audience already agrees to and may already be doing something about! Its purpose is to stimulate, to heighten, to emotionalize existent belief and action—to get people to believe more fervently and/or to perform with even greater devotion.

The best examples of the speech to actuate are the halftime spiel by the football coach to his team, the sermon, and the sales manager's pep talk to the sales staff at their regular meeting.

The coach knows the team wants to win; he knows they have been playing for a full half; and it is his unenviable task to try to get them to try even harder, to fight even more fiercely the second half. His difficult task is made even more so by the fact that the players know just exactly what he is supposed to do for them; and they have heard a lot of these locker-room harangues.

The minister knows that the church members agree to the church's dicta; knows that they give of their time and treasure to support the church; and that the purpose of sermons is to try to get the church members to believe ever more fervently and to give ever more generously. And the sermon has to be stimulating and fresh every week, fifty weeks a year. No wonder ministers move from church to church every few years. They need audiences who have not heard all their material!

The sales manager's problems are not unlike those of the coach and the minister.

Now teachers are lucky. They can keep the same old lectures because the students change regularly!

Again, the ideal tool for organizing this speech is the motivated sequence, with especially heavy emphasis on the visualization step. It is difficult; you must be stimulating yourself. And if you must give a speech to stimulate, I have very little advice for you, because to inspire, one must either be an inspired wordsmith oneself or else be able to find and use highly inspirational supporting material to cite (which is perhaps why preachers read so much?). I cannot train you to become an inspired wordsmith; you have to be born that way. But anyone can learn (or can be taught to become) a collector and user of inspirational supporting examples. *Reader's Digest* carries a lot of them, for instance. Subscribe and read it.

On Proof

Before concluding this chapter, we must briefly consider *proof*.

The Greeks of Aristotle's time divided all oratorical proof into three categories, which still hold up well today: *logos, pathos,* and *ethos.*

Logos is what we might call *logical proof* or *supporting material* or *evidence*. This is what Chapter 4 of this book is all about: that chapter tells you what kind of evidence you need to find and how to find it. You may want to review that chapter briefly. The Greeks said that *logos* resides in the speech; and that's exactly right. You go and find it and put it into the speech.

Pathos is the form of proof the Greeks saw as residing in the audience. It is the human tendency to respond to emotional appeals. If I move the audience by appeals to their pride, nationalism, greed, piety, sex drive, desire for recognition and status, and so on, I have appealed to tendencies already within my audience. *Pathos* has been the main concern of this chapter. That's what motivation is all about. If, in your persuasive speech, you do not raise the audience's blood pressure, body temperature, circulation, and respiratory rate, you have not motivated (emotionalized) them. That's what effective appeals to the emotions do.

Ethos is the form of proof that resides in the speaker; it is personal proof. If you believe (or *don't* believe!) an argument just because I was the one who brought it up, *ethos* has been at work.

Scientific factor-analytic studies have shown that *ethos* (typically called by modernists *speaker credibility*) is composed of two dependable factors: character and authoritativeness. Character can also be thought of as trustworthiness, or likability. Authoritativeness can also be thought of as expertise, competence, or capability.

Another way of dividing *ethos* is useful. Even Aristotle felt that there were two kinds of *ethos*. One kind is ascribed *ethos,* or what we might call *reputation,* which is what the audience thinks about you from before, and not from what you say in your speech. The other kind is acquired *ethos,* or what we might call *earned credibility.* This latter is the *ethos* that you earn (or fail to earn) during the speech. And even Aristotle argued that a speaker should never depend on previous reputation for any one speech but should be determined to earn credibility from what she or he says and how she or he says it in each speech. It's good advice. One airlines president says to his customers, "We have to earn our wings every day!"

Of course, if you are a beginning speaker and are not considered an expert in your topic, you will not have any strong reputation on which to depend. That means that you *must* depend on your speech, what you say and how you say it, to produce any credibility, which you must earn. What features of speaking will earn *ethos* points for you? Here the accumulated research is most informative. There are several things you can do to boost your *ethos*.

First, be and appear *sincere*. Listeners respond favorably to a speaker who appears completely sincere. This point was referred to in Chapter 7. It means that to generate credibility, you must either (1) manifest sincerity through exceptionally good acting or else (2) speak in such a way that the manifest sincerity you naturally possess cannot be hidden. As only one in a million or so is a good actor, I recommend the latter.

Another point made in Chapter 7 was that good delivery—looking and sounding good—will please and delight the audience. It will also generate credibility, studies show.

Sincerity and good delivery lead to another personal attribute that is associated with high speaker credibility: *poise*. Be poised and confident, and the audience will believe you; demonstrate excessive nervousness and lack of composure, and the audience just won't buy what you say.

A multitude of studies reflect the conclusion that the more and better the *evidence* (*logos*) you use in your speech, the more highly credible you will seem to your audience. The general response is "My, our speaker really knew that topic inside and out!"

Your general credibility is perceived as higher if the audience can also perceive that you are *impartial;* however, if they cannot perceive your impartiality (and it's hard to be impartial on a topic dear to us), they will settle for *fairness*. This is the best reason I can think of for you to know all the other sides to your proposition just as well as your own—and to acknowledge any really strong points from those sides.

Finally, research shows that a speaker who demonstrates a sense of humor is generally rated higher on the character dimension of *ethos*. If you are able to make fun of yourself and others playfully during the serious business of making a speech, you will be seen as having a balanced sense of perspective about the world. You will be seen as one who does not take life *too* seriously—and is certainly no fanatic—and is therefore liked and trusted.

A Parting Shot

I personally believe that this chapter gives you excellent advice on how to develop any kind of persuasive speech. I strongly urge that you review it before beginning work on any such speech. And as usual, I admonish you to review Chapter 2, the "blocking and tackling" chapter, before beginning work on *any* speech, persuasive or not.

10

Make Better Decisions: Get Several Heads Together

This is a chapter on group discussion or group decision-making tacked onto a primer on public speaking. "Why?" you might ask. Because it is my experience that people who become able public speakers find themselves on many decision-making boards, committees, and "task forces" for various civic, educational, business, and charitable organizations. After all, ours is a society governed by talk—mostly by committees.

Maybe you never thought of that. I emphasized in the last chapter that most of our thinking and behavior are due to emotional forces—that we do and think as we want to. But when we have a serious and important problem to solve, we generally form a committee and put several heads to work on it, employing all the logic, evidence, and common sense we can muster.

Just what do we mean by *group discussion*? Well, it is here meant as serious talk by a small group to solve a mutual problem. It is further defined as a process that relies on careful planning, is relatively informal, induces wide participation from its members, has a common purpose for all involved, and benefits from leadership. Let us look at each of these points in more detail.

Planning. Almost any problem-solving situation benefits from planning. The steps to be followed are carefully laid out in an agenda, either by a leader or by a smaller subcommittee of the whole group. Different people might be assigned to research different aspects of the problem in order to share the burden. Consideration of the problem, in the following the steps based on John Dewey's "steps in reflective thinking," is important.

Informality. The discussion should be conducted in a group small enough to converse easily and exchange ideas and information and evaluations easily, face-to-face, without the necessity of conducting the meeting under parliamentary procedure. Such a procedure becomes necessary only when a larger group considers the pros and cons of the particular solutions offered.

Participation. Wide participation aids in problem solving. The very reason for having a group, rather than one or two individuals, take up a problem for solution is that a variety of viewpoints and information sources are believed helpful. If everyone contributes, this variety obtains.

Common Purpose. The people in the group that is to solve a problem must have a common purpose or goal. Otherwise the result is factionalism, rivalry, face-saving, and friction—not cooperation. Before the proceedings start, someone should try to find out if such a commonality of purpose exists; otherwise, be prepared to agree to disagree.

Leadership. Most groups have either a designated or a natural leader. Sometimes the leader emerges during the early stages of deliberation, the group having begun without a designated leader. At other times, the leader will be appointed by an officer of the parent organization, or the group will elect its own chairman. But no matter who is the leader, the group will benefit from the leadership *functions*, and whoever *does* provide them:

1. Builds a permissive climate, so that people will feel free to contribute and evaluate information and ideas.

2. Makes sure that the plan, or agenda, is followed.

3. Occasionally gives accurate summaries or gets them from others. This summarizing helps to confirm that the group is still "together" up to that point.

4. Gives or gets clarification of any vague, ambiguous statement. Otherwise such statements, left hanging in the air, confuse.

5. Promotes evaluations of generalizations, especially broad ones: "OK, Joe, you say that last year's program was an utter failure. Maybe it was. Do *you* think so, Mary? Sam? How about you, Susan?"

6. Protects minority opinion, when voiced (otherwise, a minority of one may decide to stay clammed up): "All right, now. We know that Mitch, here, feels entirely differently from us about the whole situation. Mitch, why don't you tell us as clearly as you can what your stand is? And we'll try to give our fair consideration."

7. Minimizes *extrinsic* conflicts. Conflict over substantive issues often brings out information and ideas necessary to the solution of the problem. But conflict over something else (such as who is doing the most work in the group) is counterproductive.

8. Performs only *necessary* functions. If the leader does only what is necessary, the other members do more, and thus they become more committed to the work and the conclusions of the group.

The Discussion Process

Discussion should proceed, normally, through a six-step process, beginning with a question or problem and ending with a solution. But I wish to emphasize here that the participants must come to their task with an attitude and a spirit of *inquiry*. Each discussant's mind must be free of preconceived solutions to the problem to be discussed, for discussion is the process of *inquiry*, and it benefits from open minds. The member who comes to the task with one or more preconceived notions of what should be done (especially any *self-serving* solutions) comes with a hidden agenda that will be a constantly disrupting influence.

Step 1. Some might not include this as a "step," but I think that the first thing that must happen to get a problem-solving discussion group going is for someone to *become aware that a problem exists*—to see that something is wrong. This is sometimes referred to as the *felt-need step.*

Step 2. The problem is worded as a question. This is a very important step, because the wording of the question determines the wording of the answer, and even the way you go about answering it. Here are some "rules."

1. Make sure that each word in the question is easily definable. This means avoiding vague abstractions like *government, Big Business, labor,* and almost any word ending in *ism.*

2. Make sure the question, as worded, is *answerable.* Avoid beginning it with *why* or *should.*

3. Word the question fairly, leaving out loaded words.

4. State the question so as not to evoke a "yes" or "no" answer right away. "Should we raise dues this year" is unfortunate; "What steps can we take to raise money?" is better. Once a member says "yes" or "no," especially publicly, a commitment has been made—and a mind has become closed.

Step 3. The problem is explored. Usually the members will have researched the problem just as one would research a topic for a speech (see Chapter 4). During this step—probably the longest that your group will engage in—the information and ideas gathered will be shared and evaluated through conversation. What is the basic *nature* of the problem (is it basically economic? political? moral? social?)? What is its history? Has it been around a long time? If so, what has been done in the past to solve it? Or is it a new, perhaps unique, problem, for which a unique and creative solution must be devised? What is the extent or seriousness of the problem? Who is being hurt by it, and to what degree? And so on.

Step 4. Only after familiarizing yourselves thoroughly with the problem do you turn to the fourth step, developing criteria to apply to the eventual solution. Why do this before discussing solutions themselves? Because a discussion of solutions might, again, cause some members to voice support for one solution—thus closing their minds. On the other hand, whereas people might disagree over solutions, it is easy to get them to agree on *criteria,* such as "It must be affordable." "It must be legal, moral, constitutional." "It must be enforceable." "It must not create additional problems." "It must be acceptable to those who must carry it out and live by it." "Other things being equal, it should be the simplest." And so on.

Step 5. After compiling your list of criteria, you are ready to begin a list of possible solutions. You would probably benefit here from changing your tactics to what is called *brainstorming.* This is the technique of having the members blurt out any imaginable idea for solving the problem—no matter how illogical or wacky it sounds at first blush. The important feature of brainstorming is that such goofiness generates a large number of ideas by *not allowing any evaluation* of the ideas proposed. Thus you can be as uninhibited as possible; *your* crazy idea might be unacceptable, but it might inspire someone else to come up with a parallel or similar idea that *will* work. Brainstorming has a track record of producing large numbers of ideas.

Step 6. This is where you put your critical thinking caps back on. Evaluate the solutions on your list, in light of the criteria you decided on earlier, and adopt the best one—the one that best fits your criteria. If your criteria were selected for clarity and comprehensiveness, selecting the best solution should be easy. If some members have "hidden-agenda" solutions or criteria not yet discussed, be prepared to wrangle and tangle at this point.

These are the steps the agenda should follow. The result should be an agreed-upon solution. What now?

Ordinarily, you would take some action to implement your solution. You would leave inquiry behind and embark on advocacy. If yours is a group of "concerned citizens," you might want to contact your Senator, your state representative, your county commissioner, and so on, to urge adoption of your plan. If your group is a committee of a parent organization, your leader will report back to that larger group, probably make an oral report of your work (see pp. 121-123, Chap. 8), and end it with, "And, therefore, our committee moves that we take the following action: . . ." Now a solution is on the floor, ready for debate. Discussion, you see, begins with inquiry and ends with a solution; debate begins with a solution and argues for and against it.

Selected Research Findings

Certain generalizations about the discussion process have been supported by empirical research. This chapter would be incomplete without a brief discussion of some of the generalizations that are most important to an understanding of group problem-solving.

The importance of common goals for all members has already been mentioned. But another feature of discussion that results in success is *cohesiveness* of the members. If the members get to know one another, understand the existing power relationships, learn their own roles in the group, and learn to get along with each other, cohesiveness, or closeness, emerges—and the group becomes productive. This "getting along" is mostly achieved through what discussion experts call *group maintenance functions,* such as joking to release tension and making supporting statements, such as "I agree with you," or "That's a very good point." In other words, you maintain the group morale by being pleasant and tactful. And whenever someone tells me, "I just can't be pleasant and tactful," I have a good reply: "You can be pleasant and tactful to your boss, can't you?" When I get a "yes," I go on: "Then just pretend you are a valued *employee* of each member in your group; you'll be pleasant and tactful."

Decisions reached after discussion are likely to be superior in quality to decisions made by individuals working alone. This seems to be true if the problem is figuring out how many beans are in a jar or what kind of personnel grievance plan would best serve the company.

The one personal attribute that seems to be related to success as a discussant is *reflective thinking ability*. This trait, as measured by the Johnson Test of Reflective Thinking Ability, is mostly (as far as I can tell) an ability to draw inferences from facts and to be willing to refuse to draw such inferences if the facts are too scarce.

If a majority position becomes apparent in a group, it is likely to influence minority-opinion members in that direction; this point was mentioned earlier as a reason that a permissive climate must be maintained so that minority-opinion members will contribute. The minority of one is especially vulnerable to majority pressure; in fact, if a minority of one is not protected in terms of expressing an opinion by one other person in the group, the group is likely to expend all its energy on arguing with the minority person in order to convert her or him. If she or he fails to convert, the majority will probably simply reject the nonconformist.

This is a brief, but compact chapter. Just as we must have thousands of laws, apparently, which try to fulfill the Golden Rule, so we have here several hundred words that try to help you succeed in following another biblical dictum: "Come, let us reason together."

Sample Speeches and Outlines

The playwright's finished product is a script. But that script is not yet a *play*. To become a play, that script must be transformed by a director, a cast, and a crew into a living, breathing drama on a stage. Costumes, makeup, lighting, physical properties, and sound effects further enhance the script's vivification.

The printed manuscript of a speech, like the playwright's script, is a lifeless, pale shadow compared to the vital, animated event of the speech itself. The manuscript lacks the cadence of the speaker's rhythm and personality, the vocal stress and emphasis, the pregnant pause, the subtle (and sometimes not-so-subtle) interplay of the speaker and the audience.

This book cannot reproduce for you videotapes of sample speeches but must settle for manuscripts. However, although the vital speech events cannot be replicated here, you can learn something of the organization, language, and phrasing of successful short speeches by reading and studying the manuscripts in this appendix.

The following is a classroom speech made by Mr. Mark B. Perry in a Speech 108 course at the University of Georgia, July 19, 1979. It is edited and reprinted here by permission of Mr. Perry.

You Don't Have to Keep on Taking It

Have you ever watched a mother feeding her little baby split-pea mush—and the baby eats until it has had enough and decides to spew the green mush back all over Mommy? Well, maybe sometimes you have felt like spewing back the split-pea mush poked at you by a radio or television station. Maybe something you have heard or seen on the media really ticked you off, and you wanted to complain about it. I know that happens to me regularly. But most people never put in their complaint; they may not know just how to go about it, or they may think, "Oh, what the heck. What good would it do anyway!"

Well, I want to tell you today that you have the right and the power and the opportunity to complain *and get results* from the electronic media. And I would like to explain how to do this effectively. First, I would like to explain how the FCC—the Federal Communications Commission—operates to regulate broadcasting, and how you can use the FCC to put pressure on local broadcasters *and* networks. And then I want to explain how to get specific results in certain cases involving local stations or networks, whether you just want to ask a question or make a specific complaint.

First of all, let's suppose your complaint is a real biggie: some station or network is obviously violating its commitment to serve in the "public interest." You want to stop them. You will want to contact the Federal Communications Commission; that's the governmental agency that has sole regulatory power for granting and renewing broadcast licenses. Just as you need a license to drive a car, a broadcast station needs a license to use the airways, which belong to the public. Just as you can lose your driver's license by breaking the law, so can a station lose its broadcast license for violating regulations.

Broadcast licenses are usually routinely renewed every three years unless there is evidence that the station is not operating in the public interest. And the station is required to ascertain the needs of the community and to program to meet those needs. That's why you hear so many editorials and public service announcements on radio and TV; these are clearly "in the public interest." You can have an active role in this license renewal process.

Suppose a station in your area has too little music or too little news; maybe they have too many commercials or show obvious discriminatory practices in their hiring procedures or refuse to carry certain stories in the news because of favoritism. You can submit a petition to the FCC asking that they deny the renewal of the station's license.

What you do is gather some signatures and evidence of misconduct and send them to the FCC in Washington. They will have hearings and, in the process, consider this petition in the renewal process. If they find justification in your complaint, they will issue a cease-and-desist order; that is a temporary probation for the station warning them to clean up their act. If, during the probationary period, the station fails to correct the situation, the FCC can lift its license and award the frequency to some other individual or company. It has been done before, many times.

But maybe you don't want to go so far as to get a license suspended because a station broadcasts a lot of garbage riddled with sexual stereotyping and senseless violence. But you still would like to complain, maybe put a stop to what you feel is offensive. Well, you can still make your complaint known to the local station.

It's really a little ironic. Local stations *want* your critical letters. If you write in and complain, and the station can do something about that complaint—say, correct it completely—they will keep your letter and show it to the FCC at renewal time, along with an explanation of how they responded. It makes them look great!

So, don't hesitate to write. Get those loads off your chest, and become a mover and shaker.

Now, the key to getting your letter read by the right person is to address it to the proper individual at the station. For instance, if your complaint or question concerns overall station policy, find out the name of the general manager or the owner of the station (a simple phone call will get it) and send it to that person, in care of the station. If you are bothered by the news, send your complaint to the specific producer of the news. The point is, mail your letter to the specific individual; and above all, write "Confidential" on the envelope. That will ensure that it gets to the person's office and into that person's hands to be read. I was once troubled by a program on CBS radio. So I wrote the show's director, Mr. Andrew Rooney; I got satisfaction in a letter from Mr. Rooney almost by return mail.

Of course, now we're talking about network complaints. Here you have to remember that *you* are the lifeblood of the networks. Without an audience, ABC, NBC, CBS, PBS, and HBO have no reason to exist. So, tell 'em what you like and don't like.

Before I go into how to write your letter to the network, let me talk for a minute on how the networks handle the huge quantities of mail that come into their shops. First, it all comes into the mail-room. Here it is sorted out according to the addressee. If mail is addressed to an individual, then it's sent right to that individual's office, where it will be read either by the addressee or by his or her secretary; from here, it may go to the agency in the network best qualified to answer the question or reply to the complaint. Most letters come in addressed either to a show or just to the net-work itself. These go to an office known as the Audience Infor-mation Office. This office answers some of the letters; others they refer to another agency, just the way the individuals do.

Another important point to remember about the Audience Infor-mation Office: it occasionally reports to the network's top brass on how the mail is going. For instance, they may keep score of how the mail is running for and against a particular program or issue (like TV violence); they tally up the scores and send them up to the bosses, such as William Paley, President of CBS, who can then review them and see what the public is thinking. So, if you think that your one letter is not going to have any impact, just remember that there are probably thousands of people out there writing in on the same matter. The only way you can get your vote in is to write, yourself.

Again, the key to success is to direct your letter to the particular program, agency, or individual who can take action on your letter. If you need to learn the name of the particular individual you want to write, you can often find it in Standard and Poor's directory of U.S. businesses and corporations.

So remember, limit your complaint or query to one particular point, so that your letter can go directly to the agency that can handle it. And wherever possible, address your letter to a particular person.

Here are a few more points that might prove helpful.

State your credentials. Yes, even if you are a college student, they will listen if you tell them that. After all, the college market is a very lucrative one for the media. Also, send a copy of the letter to the sponsors of the program. They are the folks putting up the money for the program, and they don't want to offend potential customers of their products. And sponsors want to know what peo-ple think about the programming they support. You ought to send a copy of the letter, also, to the local station carrying the material, for the same reasons.

Above all, check to make sure your facts are correct; your letter should seem to be the work of an incisive, calm, knowledgeable critic or inquirer who seems to know what is really going on—you don't want your letter to go into the ash can as the work of a kook.

You, the viewer or listener, are the key to broadcasting. You can control what is being flushed into your home on the cathode ray tube. So the next time the media irk you, take action. Write that letter. You can complain or ask questions on the local level or the network level, or in extreme cases, you can even petition to deny the license of the broadcast station. After all, if the media are required to program in the public interest, the public has to be interested enough to let the broadcasters know just what *is* the public interest.

On October 17, 1980, Ms. Louise C. Hoke gave a speech in Speech 218H at the University of Georgia. The outline and the text of that speech follow; both are edited for print and are published by permission of Ms. Hoke, a freshman at the university at the time.

How To Remember What's-Her-Name

Purpose: To teach the audience how to use the principles behind one method of remembering names.

INTRODUCTION

   I. Here at school we all meet lots of people whose names we cannot remember. Right?

  II. Well, remembering those names is not so difficult if you will remember and use a simple four-step process I would like to explain.

BODY

   I. The first step in becoming a name expert is getting the name right the first time.

     A. Do not let a name slip past you in an introduction.

     B. Block out everything but the name that is being stated.

     C. If you did not understand the first time, ask for a repetition of the name.

     D. If necessary, ask for a spelling of the name.

Transition: Making sure you heard the name right at first is fine, but there is more to do.

  II. The second step is to hammer the name into your memory through repetition.

     A. Use the name as much as possible during the course of the conversation.

       1. Begin the conversation by addressing the new acquaintance by name.

       2. Precede as many sentences as possible with the new acquaintance's name.

       3. In parting, be sure to use the name in any farewell remarks.

     B. As soon as possible, write the name down for future reference.

Transition: And there's something else to do while you are repeating that name so often.

III. Fasten in your mind an image of the new acquaintance's face.
  A. During an introduction be observant of any distinguishing characteristics the person might have.
    1. Look for anything unusual first, such as scars, warts, wrinkles, or moles.
    2. Study other things, too, like ears, nose, eyes, hair, weight, and height.
  B. Do this often enough, and you will learn to be observant almost as a habit.

Transition: But there is one more thing you can do also.

IV. Finally, anchor the name through *association*.
  A. Think of anyone else you know with the same name.
  B. Concentrate on any facts you learn during a conversation that you can associate with this person.
  C. Try to connect the name with a slogan, an allusion, or a familiar quotation.
  D. Try to make a rhyme out of the name ("Here's Mr. Hummock, with a large stomach."), so that the person's appearance will suggest the name.

CONCLUSION

I. So remember to get the name right at first, to repeat it as often as possible during your conversation, to remember the face that goes with the name, and to anchor the name to your memory by association.
II. Do these four things regularly, and enjoy the most important part of college: meeting people!

How To Remember What's-Her-Name

Going to college is one great experience after another, isn't it? There are new classes, new rooms, clubs, activities, and social customs. But most important of all is new friends. And with each new friend comes one new face and one new name that make that person unique.

I know that you've each met a lot of people since coming to the University. And I am equally sure that you have forgotten many of their names already. Am I right? The faces still are familiar, maybe, but the names just won't come to mind. Well, making new friends takes time, and one way to turn acquaintances into those new friends faster is to use names. Remembering names and faces doesn't have to be hard. It just has to become more systematic. Today I would like to explain a simple four-step process that will help you put names and faces together. First, you have to get the name right in the first place. Second, you hammer the name in by repetition. Third, you fasten the image of the face in your mind. And fourth, you anchor the name through association.

The first step is to get the name straight right off the bat. This is probably the easiest of all the four steps. In an introduction, don't let a name just slip past you. Very often the person making the introductions knows both names so well that the names will be zipped hurriedly through or badly slurred, and you won't quite catch it. So if you don't hear the name well, be sure to speak up. Say, "I'm sorry—I didn't hear the name. Could you repeat it?" Usually, when you do this, the person you just met will be flattered because you are interested enough to inquire about his or her name. You are *interested* in this person. Of course, often the other person will respond with, "Well, I didn't catch yours either." And so mutual respect is established.

Another important thing to remember at this point is to block out mentally everything but the name that you are hearing. Concentrate! Often you will be so wrapped up in the sight of the person you are meeting that you'll forget to listen for the name—you'll just not be paying any attention. So be sure to wait until that name has sunk into your head before you begin to notice what the person is wearing or looks like or anything else. And don't be distracted by listening to see if your name has been pronounced correctly. That can be cleared up later, if necessary. Listen for the other's name. Don't just hang back, expecting to catch it later in the conversation, because it may never happen. Speak up if you don't hear it well; getting that name right to begin with is absolutely essential, and it's the easiest step of all.

OK, now, after hearing that name correctly in the first place, move on to the second step, which is to hammer the name in by repetition. This means simply thinking about the name as much as possible, saying it as much as you can in conversation, and listening every time the name is used. An easy way to do this is to use the person's name in the first statement you make after being introduced. Say, "Hello, George," or "Hello, Sarah," along with "It's so nice to meet you." Use that name. From then, on use it as much as you can, in every sentence. People *love* to hear their own names in someone else's discourse!

Now, if you are with a big bunch of people, this might be kind of hard to do. But you need to use the name at the ends of sentences, in the middle, and wherever else you can. Don't make it too obvious, but still use it often, so that the name sinks into your brain. And if you *are* in a large group and don't have a lot of time to talk and say that new name, just repeat it to yourself silently three or four times. This helps a lot.

Finally, when you are getting ready to leave, think about all the times you have left someone and he or she has said, "Well, sure nice to meetcha," without your name. They've forgotten it. Then you say this: "Well, it was certainly nice to meet you, Harold (or whatever), and I hope to see you again soon." Do this, and Harold will be flattered—and truly interested in seeing you again soon, too.

Another trick used by many is to write the name down, especially if it is an unusual name or has an unusual spelling. And it's a good idea to have someone spell his or her name during the introductions if the name is unusual. I read once about a businessman who ran into an old customer on the commuter train, but he could not for the life of him remember the customer's name. During the conversation, the customer said that the businessman should call him soon for a new order. The businessman became desperate over the customer's name. Finally, he said, "I need to write down your name, but I want to be sure it is spelled correctly. Could you spell out your name for me?" The *former* customer replied icily, "Sure. It's B - O - B Bob. S - M - I - T - H." So be careful about the spelling bit. You have been warned.

But this writing the name down works. That's a technique that Napoleon III used. When he first got into power, he needed the support of all his subjects. He figured a good way to get it would be to learn as many names as possible. So whenever he met someone, he would write the name on a little piece of paper as soon as he could, and he would then sit and look at it for a few minutes. And it worked for him like a fine watch.

Salespeople use this technique also. People successful in sales write down and file away the names not only of their clients but of their secretaries and other employees. They know that remembering the receptionist's name is a real plus in getting in quickly to see the boss, and that knowing and using the names of the store's sales force will make them enthusiastic in pushing the sales representative's particular brand of merchandise.

Well, now, steps one and two help you learn and remember names. Step three helps you put the names with the faces; it helps by fastening the faces in your mind. So after that name has been heard correctly, and as you are using it as much as you can in conversation, start becoming observant of the person you just met. Remembering faces is not a matter of eyesight but of careful observation.

An important element of careful observation is *calm*. Be calm. I know it's difficult sometimes, in the flush and excitement of meeting a new potential friend, but you have to practice. Look at the face. Study it. Are there any unusual features, like scars, moles, or warts? Any wrinkles, red hair, or anything else that stands out? After the unusual things, start taking in the more common things, like hair color, weight, age, voice, stance, the way of walking or talking—the arrangement of facial features, like eyes, ears, nose, mouth—anything like that.

Now, being observant is a useful but not an easy-to-acquire trait. If you are not a really observant person, you need to train yourself and to make being observant more or less a habit. Most police officers become unusually observant through training and motivation, as do the President's Secret Service men. You can practice being observant of people anywhere: walking down the street, riding a bus, just about anywhere. Glance at a face, then close your eyes (or, look away), and then try to reconstruct a picture of that face in your mind. Then check the face with another glance.

At a movie, try to learn as many names of the actors and actresses as possible, and not only their names, but the names of the characters they played also. This is excellent practice. And practice is what you need in order to develop the habit of observation. And once you have this habit of observation, you will be surprised at how many things you notice about people that you never noticed before.

The fourth and final step is to anchor the name by association. You need to try to link that name to as many related impressions and facts as you can, so that later on it will just pop right back into your head.

Now, there are several methods you can use to do this. First of all, say to yourself, "Do I know anyone else by that name?" It doesn't have to be a close friend or a relative. It can be a politician, or a movie star, or some famous person in history. Just associate that new name with the other person, and it will help loads—especially if the two persons share some likenesses.

Also, associate something about the person's name with something you know or learn about him or her. For instance, you meet a Mr. Parr; then you find out he is a golfer. Parr, par. This should be easy. Or you meet a Mrs. Cobb. Think of her as eating corn on the *cob.* You meet an older man, say, a Mr. Sands. You can associate his name with the sands of time. Associate a name with something that rhymes. You meet a Mr. Hughes, who is chewing gum. "Mr. Hughes *chews,*" you say to yourself. Just the fact that you have taken the extra mental effort to make some association of this kind will cement the name more firmly in your skull.

Of course, associations can trip you up, sometimes, too. A man met a rather portly woman named Mrs. Hummock. He thought he could remember her name easily by associating her name with her round, protruding abdomen. "Hummock, stomach," he thought.

Weeks later, however, he met her in the supermarket. "Good afternoon, Mrs. Kelly," he smiled.

You also need to realize that you can help others remember *your* name by using similar techniques. Ralph, here, could tell people he meets, "My name's Ralph. You know, how the dog barks in the old Pogo strip: 'Ralph, Ralph!' " Mr. Gruner told me about a retired dentist he met down at Jekyll Island who said, "Name's Quiggle. Rhymes with 'wiggle.' "! And I imagine lots of his patients *did* wiggle!

So there you have it. There are four basic steps to remembering names and faces. Get the name straight the first time. Hammer that name in by repetition. Fasten the face in your mind. Then anchor the name by association. Practicing these four steps can make your boring life exciting. So put them to work for you, and enjoy one of the most important aspect of college life: meeting people.

The University of Georgia operates a banking school through the Continuing Education Center. For two weeks during each of three years, bank employees hone their knowledge and skills in banking and finance; they also study public speaking.

The following is a speech presented in that school by Ms. Sandra G. Smith on May 19, 1980. The speech has been edited and is printed here by permission of Ms. Smith, an employee of the Bank of Dade, Trenton, Georgia.

You've Come A Long Way, Baby, but . . .

Thanks to the Virginia Slims ads we're all familiar with the phrase, "You've come a long way, baby." And that's a very true statement. Women *have* come a long way. But that coming has been a long, drawn-out process, and frankly, women haven't fully arrived yet, either. For years women have tried to convince the world that they are more than just "stay-at-home, do-nothing-all-day squaws." Of course, even when we stay home, we don't exactly just "do nothing." Back in 1897 a piece appeared in a magazine called *The Garden and Farm Journal* that directly related to this issue. This short article, entitled "The Industrious Woman," presented some statistics on how the average Michigan woman used up her time at home: "A Michigan woman made 191 pies, 140 cakes, 84 loaves of bread, 729 biscuits, 156 fried cakes and 1026 cookies in her statistical year, which ended September 1." And this was in addition to caring for her children and doing her regular housework. This information may aid those men who wonder whatever it is that a woman does with all her time back in the little cottage.

Well, I don't know how convincing that article was to the male population back in 1897, but I'm glad that a woman's success today isn't dependent on the amount of baking she does in a year. Today women are able to compete much more fairly in work situations with men, and they are proving themselves to be both capable and efficient. This opportunity, never thought possible before, is the result of such things as federal legislation decrees, equal pay and equal credit, and a rapid increase in the number of women in the work force. Last, but not least, is the women's liberation movement.

Now, don't get me wrong. I do *not* count myself as a hard-line "women's libber." I appreciate very much the traditional and biological differences between men and women. In fact, I like to repeat a little couplet I ran across in *Reader's Digest* not long ago. It goes:

Women, it now appears, are very much like men,
Except, of course, for here and there, and sometimes now and
then.

In other words, I don't think *equality* need get confused with
any sense of *superiority*. The point of the women's movement that
I *do* support is equal opportunity for equally qualified people,
whether male or female. This is something that is becoming more
and more accepted, especially in the business world. According to
the most recent figures available from the Bureau of Labor Statistics, 27.3 percent of the nation's banking officials and financial
managers are now women. That's not bad, and another proof that
we HAVE come a long way.

The most fascinating thing about the whole subject, though, is
that women are gaining this right to prove themselves not because
men are giving it to them, but because they are giving it to themselves. By this I mean that women's support of other women has
become the catalyst for the movement. We don't see this yet as
much in our geographical area as in other parts of the country,
because although it might kind of hurt our pride to admit it, the
South tends to lag a little behind some other areas in accepting
some trends. Patricia Scott, management consultant for the National Association of Bank Women, Incorporated, says that in her
dealings with women bankers she is finding that more and more
they are beginning to support each other. It can be in just little
ways—as simple as not being overly critical of each other. I am
sure that right now possibly many of you sitting there think that
the women that I know and work with certainly haven't learned to
stop being so critical of one another. I would have to agree with
you, too, and that is what I mean when I say we tend to lag behind
some other parts of the country.

It is a bitter dose of medicine for us gals to swallow, but the fact
is, we women are often our own worst enemies. Maybe you men
here have been accused of male chauvinism. And maybe those
charges are a little justified? If so, you deserve anything you get,
for my money. But even if we women don't have to cope with male
chauvinists in our place of work, even if we get solid support from
the men working around and with us, we still have serious problems without the support of other women.

Quite frankly, I think that both sexes will benefit when women
learn this lesson in "self-support." Can you ladies here imagine
being told that you are getting a promotion, and taking that news
without a sudden, funny little feeling deep down in the pit of your
stomach that there are going to be other women in the bank that
are going to get mad at you for getting that promotion? In such a

situation, I think, some men might also be envious and jealous of the woman's promotion, but they cover up these feelings much better than other women. Not that men just have a different emotional makeup than us women; I think it's just that women are relative newcomers to the business world, and, as tyros, we have not had as much time as men have had to learn the ropes, to absorb and follow the ethics of the business place.

I saw something on the local Chatthanooga television news a few weeks ago that shows that that area, which is my home stomping grounds, has quite a way to go as far as support among women is concerned. This was during National Secretaries Week, and the reporter was interviewing a woman who worked for one of the area's leading industries. She very emphatically stated that she would rather work for a man than for a woman! According to her, it "just didn't seem right" to work for a woman. Now, if she had been a true supporter of other females, she would never have admitted this, even if she believed it. Can you imagine a man going on TV and saying that he would prefer a woman for a boss over a man? If so, I would like to speak to you after this speech session about a little bridge I have for sale—in Brooklyn.

Even in my own bank I know of a situation that shows lack of woman-to-woman support. We have two senior officers, and they are of equal rank as far as the corporate structure chart goes. One officer is male, the other female. But if you ask the women in our bank to rank our officers, every one will rank the male higher than the female. Now, this is not the guy's fault; it's just the trend of thinking among women in this area of the country. Obviously, our bank is not what Miss Scott was talking about.

I said earlier that women have come a long way but still have a way to go. Sally Buck, President of the Women's Bank of Richmond, Virginia, has expressed this same belief. She says: "There's no going back. Women are going to play a larger and larger role. It's going to be quite a while, though, before we are complete equals with men." In order to get there from here, though, it's the women as well as the men who are going to have to have their ways of thinking completely overhauled. Until women learn to accept and support other women, we are asking too much of the men when we expect *them* to do so. Now, we aren't going to let you guys off the hook completely, but we women with open minds realize that women, themselves, are responsible for part of our dilemma. So we women will accept *half* the blame for our equality problem. If women want to *have* equality, they are going to have to start to *think* equality, *believe* equality, and to *behave* equality. After all, equality is what it's all about. As Ashley Montagu once wrote, "It is the mark of the cultured man that he is aware of the fact that equality is an ethical and not a biological principle."

The following speech was presented by Mr. Jack H. Kirkman, a freshman student at the University of Georgia, during fall quarter of 1980. It is edited for print and printed here by permission of Mr. Kirkman.

With Speed in the Dark

All of you here have seen *Gone with the Wind,* right? Well, in *Gone with the Wind* you get that picture of Clark Gable, blockade runner, as he walks through the big dance, with his white suit, white Panama hat, and Havana cigar. He's making loads of money by profiteering off the fall of the South. Unfortunately, this is the only view that most people have of Confederate blockade running, and, just as unfortunately, this view is totally false. So today I am going to give you a little background on Civil War blockade running. I recently did a term paper on the subject, and I found it fascinating. I hope you do, too.

On April 19, 1861, which was five days after the fall of Fort Sumter, Abraham Lincoln issued a proclamation saying that the North would blockade all the southern ports. Now there were two important aspects of this proclamation: number one was that a nation only blockades the ports of an *enemy nation;* therefore the North had in effect recognized the South as a belligerent. And as a belligerent, the South's side received certain rights under international law. And the second important point was the use of the word *blockade* itself. According to the Treaty of Paris, which the United States had signed, the blockade was not to be taken seriously unless it was effective. In other words, it was legal for ships of other nations to run the blockade as long as they weren't caught.

Now, this legality allowed Great Britain to perform a major role in the blockade running. As a matter of fact, the British did about 70 to 75 percent of it. There were very few actual Confederate blockade runners. This can't be underestimated—the role that Great Britain played. Her textile mills needed the South's cotton, and her factories could supply the South with most of its arms, equipment, and other hard goods. In fact, when the blockade running was finally shut down, when the last port was effectively closed, the war was over within four months. There was just nothing left for the South to fight with.

When Lincoln issued his proclamation, there were only *four* federal ships in any position to enforce the blockade, and there were four thousand miles of coastline to blockade, both the Atlantic and the Gulf coasts. So from the beginning, the blockade was, in fact, a farce. By 1862, however, the federals had recalled their ships from foreign waters and had raised the level of the blockade from a farce to that of a rough joke. Then, by 1863, they began to put some real teeth into the blockade. It became no longer profitable or possible for the blockade runners to use their large, heavy, deep-draft steamers direct from Great Britain to ply the blockaded southern ports. What they needed were small, light, fast ships.

Smaller ships meant they would have to transship the materials. And to facilitate this transshipment, they used the British colonies of Nassau and Bermuda. They'd use Nassau for running in to Savannah and Charleston, and Bermuda for running in to Wilmington, because these islands were close to the respective Confederate ports. They used Wilmington more than any other because it was easy to slip into and had a much larger outlet, and the waters were trickier for the federals to navigate with their big men-of-war. So a typical blockade runner would form a cycle: from Bermuda to Wilmington with the war materials, and then from Wilmington back to Bermuda with a load of cotton.

At this time, cotton could be purchased in the South at around six cents a pound, whereas it could be resold in Great Britain for around fifty to sixty cents a pound, creating an enormous profit. So blockade runners would put as much cotton as they could on the ships. They would totally fill up the hold, and then actually stack it too high on the deck. The bales of cotton had already been compressed to half their normal size by steam presses on the southern coast. So they would actually work the ship from an artificial deck made up of bales of cotton. Now, in this way, depending on the size of the steamer, they could get between six hundred and twelve hundred bales of cotton on board. Therefore an average ship could make a profit of maybe $420,000 off the cotton run out alone. Once in Bermuda, they would unload the cotton, take on coal, water, and provisions, and load up the ship with war materials. Now came the trickiest part of it, and that was running the material back in past the blockade warships.

The three keys to running safely into the southern ports were: (1) invisibility; (2) speed; and (3) knowledge of the coast.

First, let's consider invisibility. For their size, these ships were extremely long, about 180 feet long, and only about 20 feet wide in the beam. And they were built very close to the water. The decks rose only about 8 feet above the water. There were hardly any masts or smokestacks to speak of; these were kept very short. And so the result was long, small, low ship that had a very small wheelhouse atop it. The blockade runners didn't want to be spotted easily at all, under sea conditions. They painted the ships gray, the exact shade being obtained by experience with the sea in that area. The crew wore gray, also. Their clothes were specifically woven and dyed for the purpose on the islands of Bermuda and Nassau. And, of course, no lights were allowed on deck. A properly camouflaged blockade runner was not visible from a range of seventy-five yards on a dark night. And, indeed, it was quite common for the runners to pass the Federal blockade squadrons within a hundred yards of their ships.

OK, so these runners were practically invisible; now let's consider their speed.

These slim, low ships *were* speedy. They would run between fourteen and twenty-two knots an hour, which was a fantastic rate for those times and isn't bad even today. And the federals had no ships that could go that fast. The runners would just scoot right past the big battlewagons.

So invisibility and speed were vital to the blockade runners. But so was their knowledge of the coast. This was extremely important because they ran in on pitch-black nights. They would choose a night of no moon, preferably even a foggy or stormy night. The Carolina coast in this section is extremely flat, with no rocks and no landmarks. The pilot had to know the area like the back of his hand.

The method was to run in north of the inlet, turn parallel to the shore, and hug the shore all the way into port—and I mean *hug* the shore! Even though these ships ran six hundred to eight hundred tons, their draft was only four to eleven feet. They would actually run inside the first line of breakers, because the coast drops off rather steeply there. They would steam along just about seventy yards or so off the shore; and they would run on into the port around the end of the federal blockade squadron.

With these three elements mastered—invisibility, speed, and knowledge of the coast—the blockade runners were very rarely caught. And on their first voyage, they could realize a profit of about 125 percent on their investment, even including the cost of building the blockade-running ship. And from then on the amount of money they could make became much higher, of course, with each successful return trip. So you can see from the actual numbers what a big business it really was. In the port of Wilmington they did about $150 million worth of goods on that one end alone. And that was on the gold standard, not the Confederate money standard. To illustrate what that means in terms of what the Confederacy could buy, in one month, from one island (Nassau), to one port, Wilmington, they ran in over 130,000 rifles alone, not to mention all the other war materials and other hard goods.

So blockade running, mostly by British ships, was extremely profitable and overwhelmingly successful, as long as those three important factors were mastered: invisibility, speed, and knowledge of the coast. It was not until the blockade became nearly 100 percent effective that the supply of materials to the South was choked off, bringing an end to the Confederacy's ability to fight on.

Here is the outline for a speech presented in class by Ms. Kathy Brown February 12, 1980, at the University of Georgia. It is edited and printed here by permission of Ms. Brown.

Diabetes Mellitus

Specific Purpose: To familiarize the audience with diabetes and its symptoms, and to stress the fact that diabetes can be controlled so that its victims can lead normal lives.

INTRODUCTION

I. "You're a diabetic"—three little words from a doctor that change the lives of millions.
  A. How can this affect you?
  B. It probably doesn't now, but it could easily affect you, a best friend, or a relative in the near future.
  C. Scientists now hypothesize that diabetes may be caused by a virus and is not strictly an inherited disease.
II. Today I hope to enlarge your understanding of the disease called *diabetes*.
  A. I will explain what diabetes is.
  B. I will discuss the symptoms of diabetes.
  C. And I will tell you how a diabetic controls his or her disease.

BODY

I. First of all, just what *is* diabetes? Well, it is basically an abnormal amount of sugar in the bloodstream and the urine of the victim.
  A. The excess sugar results from the failure of the pancreas to secrete enough of the hormone insulin.
  B. Insulin helps the body to store and use sugar, and without it sugar accumulates in the bloodstream and spills into the urine.

Transition: Now that you have an idea of what diabetes is, let's look at some of the symptoms of diabetes.
II. The symptoms of diabetes are easily recognized.
  A. One symptom, for instance, is great thirst.
  B. Another is frequent and excessive urination.
    1. The body recognizes this excess of sugar in the blood.
    2. So the natural reaction is excessive urination to rid the body of the sugar.
  C. The onslaught of diabetes causes a very rapid loss in weight.

D. Another symptom is loss of strength; you just "don't feel good," and you experience that "rundown feeling."

Transition: The diabetic cannot compensate for the excess sugar all alone and needs help to control the condition.

III. Diabetes is controlled by medication, special diet, regular exercise, and a certain amount of record keeping.

    A. A diabetic must receive daily injections of insulin because the pancreas does not supply it.

    B. The diabetic must follow a special diet.

       1. The diet is administered by the physician and varies according to the amount of insulin injected daily.

       2. The diet may be changed as the diabetic condition changes.

    C. Regular exercise is prescribed according to diet and insulin dosage.

    D. A diabetic should also check his or her urine sugar level and keep a daily record of it.

CONCLUSION

  I. So remember, diabetes is excess sugar that the body can't cope with.

 II. Its symptoms are great thirst, frequent and excessive urination, rapid weight loss, and a big drop in strength and energy.

III. But a diabetic can control the disease through medication, diet, exercise, and careful self-monitoring.

IV. I myself have grown so accustomed to being a diabetic that it seems almost a "normal" state.

For the assigned "speech to actuate," Ms. Julie Wilhoit made the following speech in class on November 16, 1979, at the University of Georgia. It is edited and printed here with the permission of Ms. Wilhoit.

The VERY Special Olympics

Have you ever held a finish line? Well, I have, and I can say that it was one of the most enjoyable, rewarding, and exciting experiences that I've had. Now, I know you're probably wondering what's so great about holding a finish line. But it was a great experience for me because I held it for the handicapped kids in the Special Olympics. And at the finish line you don't really realize it, but you see all their expressions of happiness from achieving success, not necessarily from winning but just being able to cross that line. And I got to see it all. That was the first Special Olympics that I volunteered for, four years ago. And every year since then, I've been an active volunteer.

For those of you who may not be aware of what the Special Olympics is, it's simply an olympics for the handicapped. The events include track and field, swimming, gymnastics, diving, hockey, soccer, volleyball, wheelchair events, basketball, and frisbee. Today I am challenging you to become a volunteer for the Special Olympics.

There are several reasons that I feel you need to become a volunteer for the Special Olympics. First, the Special Olympics simply need your help as a volunteer. Much time and effort go into the organization of these games, and there are numerous jobs that depend on volunteers to be done. The second reason is that you need to volunteer in order to give the handicapped a chance to gain your respect as fellow human beings. Last, you need to volunteer for your own personal satisfaction. You'll learn about the handicapped in many ways. You will gain insight into the obstacles that they face every day, and that they overcome because of their sheer determination and courage. So I've said that you need to volunteer for three reasons: first, the Special Olympics needs your help; second, you need to give the handicapped this chance of gaining your respect; and third, you need to volunteer for your own personal satisfaction.

Now, I know that besides explaining why you need to volunteer, I have to go further, because when we're asked to do things we are not accustomed to doing, we develop hangups. So I'm going to try to get these hangups out in the open.

The first one is that you may be afraid of the handicapped. I'm not blaming you for any of your beliefs, but I know that many of you have probably grown up thinking that the handicapped are monsters, wierdos, creeps, and nuts. But they're not. They're just like you and me. The only thing different is that some of *their* uniqueness is a little bit more noticeable than ours. We all have our exceptionalities.

Another hangup that you may have is feeling sorry for the handicapped. You may think that if you go out and volunteer for the Special Olympics, you're going to cry all day. Well, the Special Olympics doesn't need your pity and doesn't want it. Just treat the people the way you would treat a friend. I really get tired of hearing people say, "I don't see how you can stand working with them" and "I feel so sorry for them." As far as I am concerned that's not an excuse for not volunteering for the Special Olympics.

Another big hangup that we all have concerning almost *everything* we do is pure, downright laziness. You might think that it takes a lot of preparation to go out and volunteer for the Special Olympics. But you don't do anything before that day, really. Maybe you have to spend two minutes of your time, and that's to call the director to find out where you meet on the day of the Special Olympics. Then all you have to do is just go there and get your assignment and do what you're supposed to do. So now you know that being afraid of the handicapped, feeling sorry for them, and being lazy are no excuses for not volunteering for the Special Olympics.

So where do you go to find information? I'll tell you. To find out about the Special Olympics, you can go to one of three places. First, right here on campus, you have the Student Council for Exceptional Children, the SCEC, and they are located on the fifth floor in the Aderhold Building. You will be able to find it easily; there are signs on the fifth floor. They'll be able to supply you with information. Second, the local training centers for mental retardation, such as the Mental Retardation Center here in Athens on Prince Street and the Athens Group Home for Mentally Retarded Men, will be able to supply you with information. And last, you can go to any public school and they should also be able to tell you the date and how to get in touch with the director.

So if you do not volunteer for the Special Olympics, you will not be giving the handicapped a chance to gain your respect. You will not increase your knowledge concerning the handicapped (and in this case, ignorance is *not* bliss), would be too bad because in order to make a better society, we have to get involved with each other and find out about each other. The Special Olympics gives us this chance to get involved.

In addition, if you don't become a volunteer, you will not experience some of the really special experiences that I've been fortunate enough to have myself. The Special Olympics is just like the big one. You have a parade, you get to march around with your banners, and then there's the lighting of the torch, and the track runner runs around the track and runs up the steps and lights the torch. It's all really dramatic. Now, for the very first Olympics that I worked in, as I said, I held the finish line. But in addition, one of my jobs was also to be in charge of the kids from one of the elementary schools, so when the bus drove up, I went to get them. It was Farber School—just a little old country school. Well, this little boy in my group, grabbed my hand right when he got off the bus. It was as if he needed my support. He whispered in my ear, "Will you stay with me?" and I said, "Yeah, Johnny, I'll be with you, all through the day." Well, when I wasn't holding the finish line, I was over where he was, making sure everything was going all right for him. Then, at the end of the day, when the Farber School kids were getting ready to leave, I went to tell them all good-bye, and he said "Will you walk me out to my bus?" I said, "Sure, let's go," and we went out to the bus. He was so little that I picked him up and put him on the steps of the bus. And he looked at me and hugged my neck real tight and said "I love you, Julie." And I said, "I love you too, Johnny." And I ran back toward the stadium and shed a few tears.

If you don't volunteer, you won't experience any of this. On the other hand, if you do volunteer, you will feel so good and you will have so much fun that you'll want to do it again. You will be showing that you care about the handicapped, and caring is one of the most important things in life. You will also look forward to those Special Olympics coming in future years. And you will feel good about yourself. So, again, I challenge you to volunteer for the Special Olympics.

The purpose of PLAIN PUBLIC SPEAKING was to present the information necessary in a succinct, "bare-bones" manner. For the interested reader additional books are here listed. The first group of books take the "fundamentals" type of approach in which the theory and practice of communication, both "public" and "interpersonal," are taken up, along with, usually small group communication. The second list are, for the most part, books in "advanced" public speaking.

Fundamentals of Speech Communication

BAIRD, A. CRAIG; KNOWER, FRANKLIN H., and BECKER, SAMUEL L. *Essentials of General Speech Communication,* 4/e, New York: McGraw-Hill Book Company, Publishers, 1973.

BERKO, ROY M., ANDREW D. WOLVIN and DARLYN R. WOLVIN. *Communicating: A Social and Career Focus.* Boston: Houghton Mifflin Company, 2nd Ed.

BOOK, CASSANDRA L. et al. *Human Communication: Principles, Contexts, and Skills;* New York: St. Martin's Press, 1980.

BORMANN, ERNEST G. & BORMANN, NANCY C. *Speech Communication: A Basic Approach,* 3rd Ed. New York: Harper & Row, Publishers. 1980.

BROOKS, WILLIAM D. *Speech Communication,* 4th. Dubuque, IA: Wm. C. Brown Company Publishers, 1981.

BURGOON, MICHAEL; RUFFNER, MICHAEL. *Human Communication;* 2/e. New York: Holt, Rinehart and Winston. 1978.

CIVIKLY, JEAN M. *Contexts of Communication.* New York: Holt, Rinehart and Winston. 1981.

CRAGAN, JOHN F. and DAVID W. WRIGHT. *Introduction to Speech Communication.* Prospect Heights, Illinois. Waveland Press, Inc., 1980.

DEVITO, JOSEPH A. *Communicology: An Introduction to the Study of Human Communication.* New York: Harper & Row, Publishers, 1978.

GRUNER, CHARLES R., CAL LOGUE, DWIGHT L. FRESHLEY, and RICHARD C. HUSEMAN. *Speech Communication in Society,* 2nd ed. (Boston: Allyn and Bacon, Inc., 1977.

HANCE, KENNETH G., DAVID C. RALPH, and MILTON J. WIKSELL.

Principles of Speaking, 3rd. Belmont, CA: Wadsworth Publishing Co., 1975.

HASTING, JOHN. *The Audience, The Message, The Speaker*. 2/e. New York: McGraw-Hill Book Company, Publishers, 1976.

HOPPER, ROBERT and WHITEHEAD, JACK L., JR. *Communication Concepts and Skills*. New York: Harper & Row, Publishers, 1979.

JABUSCH, DAVID M. and STEPHEN W. LITTLEJOHN. *Elements of Speech Communication: Achieving Competency*. Boston: Houghton Mifflin Company, 1981.

MCAULEY, JACK G. *People to People: Essentials of Personal and Public Communication*. Belmont, CA: Wadsworth Publishing Co., 1979.

MONROE, ALAN H. et al. *Principles and Types of Speech Communication*, 8th ed. Glenview: Scott, Foresman and Company, 1978.

MONROE, ALAN H., EHNINGER, DOUGLAS, and GRONBECK, BRUCE E. *Principles of Speech Communication*, 8th Brief ed.: Glenview: Scott, Foresman and Company, 1980.

MYERS, MICHELE T. and MYERS, GAIL E. *Communicating When We Speak*, 2/e. New York: McGraw-Hill Book Company, Publishers, 1978.

MYERS, GAIL E. and MYERS, MICHELE T. *The Dynamics of Human Communication*, 3/e. New York: McGraw-Hill Book Company, Publishers, 1980.

PEARSON, JUDY C. and NELSON, PAUL E. *Understanding and Sharing: An Introduction to Speech Communication*. Dubuque, IA: Wm. C. Brown Company Publishers, 1979.

SATHRÉ, FREDA et al. *Let's Talk: An Introduction to Interpersonal Communication*, 3rd ed. Glenview: Scott, Foresman and Company, 1981.

SCHEIDEL, THOMAS M. *Speech Communication and Human Interaction*, 2nd ed. Glenview: Scott, Foresman and Company, 1976.

SCHIFF et al. *Communication Strategy: A Guide to Speech Preparation*. Glenview: Scott, Foresman and Company, 1981.

SPROULE, J. MICHAEL *Communication Today*. Glenview: Scott, Foresman and Company, 1981.

VERDERBER, RUDOLPH F. *Communicate!*, 3rd. Belmont, CA: Wadsworth Publishing Co., 1981.

VERDERBER, RUDOLPH F. *The Challenge of Effective Speaking*, 4th. Belmont, CA: Wadsworth Publishing Co., 1979.

ZIMMERMAN, GORDON I. et al. *Speech Communication: A Contemporary Introduction*. St. Paul: West Publishing Company, 1980.

Public Speaking

ANDERSEN, MARTIN P., NICHOLAS, E. RAY JR., and BOOTH, HERBERT W. *The Speaker and His Audience: Dynamic Interpersonal Communication,* 2nd ed.: New York: Harper & Row, Publishers, 1974.

BAIRD, JOHN E. *Speaking for Results: Communication by Objectives.* New York: Harper & Row, Publishers, 1980.

BARRETT, HAROLD. *Practical Uses of Speech Communication* 5/e. New York: Holt, Rinehart and Winston, 1981.

BARRETT, HAROLD. *Speaking Practically.* New York: Holt, Rinehart and Winston, 1981.

BRADLEY, BERT E. *Fundamentals of Speech Communication: The Credibility of Ideas,* 3rd. Dubuque, IA: Wm. C. Brown Company Publishers, 1981.

CARLILE, CLARK S. *Project Text for Public Speaking,* 4th Ed. New York: Harper & Row, Publishers. 1981.

CARLSON, KAREN and MEYERS, ALAN. *Speaking with Confidence.* Glenview: Scott, Foresman and Company, 1977.

COHEN, EDWIN. *Speaking the Speech.* New York: Holt, Rinehart and Winston. 1980.

DeVITO, JOSEPH. *The Elements of Public Speaking.* New York: Harper & Row Publishers, 1980.

GARNER, DWIGHT L. *Idea to Delivery,* 3rd Belmont, CA: Wadsworth Publishing Co., 1979.

GRONBECK, BRUCE E. *The Articulate Person: A Guide to Everyday Public Speaking* Glenview: Scott, Foresman and Company, 1979.

JEFFERY, ROBERT C., and PETERSON, OWEN. *Speech: A Basic Text.* New York: Harper & Row, Publishers, 1977.

JEFFERY, ROBERT C. and PETERSON, OWEN. *Speech: A Text with Adapted Readings,* 3rd Ed. New York: Harper & Row, Publishers, 1980.

LOGUE, CAL M., DWIGHT L. FRESHLEY, CHARLES R. GRUNER, and RICHARD C. HUSEMAN, *Speaking: Back to Fundamentals,* 3rd ed. (Boston: Allyn and Bacon, Inc., 1982).

MINNICK, WAYNE C. *Public Speaking.* Boston: Houghton Mifflin Company, 1979.

MONROE, ALAN H. et al. *Principles and Types of Speech Communication,* 8th ed. Glenview: Scott, Foresman and Company, 1978.

NELSON, PAUL and PEARSON, JUDY. *Confidence in Public Speaking.* Dubuque, IA: Wm. C. Brown Company Publishers, 1981.

PETERSEN, BRENT D. et al. *Speakeasy: An Introduction to Public Speaking.* St. Paul: West Publishing Company, 1980.

REID, LOREN. *Speaking Well,* 3/e. New York: McGraw-Hill Book Company, Publishers, 1977.

REIN, IRVING J. *The Public Speaking Book.* Glenview: Scott, Foresman and Company, 1981.

RODMAN, GEORGE. *Public Speaking: An Introduction to Message Preparation,* 2/e. New York: Holt, Rinehart and Winston. 1981.

SAMOVAR, LARRY A. and MILLS, JACK. *Oral Communication: Message and Response,* 4th. Dubuque, IA: Wm. C. Brown Company Publishers, 1980.

SCHEIDEL, THOMAS N. *Persuasive Speaking.* Glenview: Scott, Foresman and Company, 1967.

THOMPSON, WAYNE N. *Responsible and Effective Communication.* Boston: Houghton Mifflin Company, 1978.